Thanks to all at Browns!
From Paul Winter
June 2003

REDSTONE

Research and design: Julian Rothenstein

Texts: Mel Gooding

Consultant: Lutz Becker

Artwork: Terence Smiyan, Marit Münzberg

Production: Tim Chester

Printed and bound by South Sea International Press, Hong Kong

First published by Redstone Press 2003
7a St Lawrence Terrace, London W10 5SU
www.redstonepress.co.uk

ISBN 1 870003 33 0

A CIP catalogue record for this book is available from the British Library.

This book is dedicated to Eric Ayers.

Grateful acknowledgment is made to the following:

Merrill C. Berman, Jim Frank
The Merrill C. Berman Collection, New York

PhDr Iva Janáková, PhDr Koenigsmarkova, Alena Zapletalová
The Museum of Decorative Arts, Prague

Kerstin Hinkel, Norbert Kaut
The Gutenberg-Museum, Mainz

Dr. Stefan Soltek, Martina Weisz
The Klingspoor Museum, Offenbach

Bertram Schmidt-Friderichs, Brigitte Raab
Verlag Hermann Schmidt, Mainz

Nigel Roache, Denise Roughan
St Bride's Printing Library, London

Pauline Rae, Jeremy Aynsley
The Royal College of Art, London

Martin Andrews
Department of Typography and Graphic Communication at
The University of Reading, Middlesex

David Batterham
David Batterham Rare Books, London

Xavier Bermúdez
Trama Visual, Mexico City

David Hillman, Sally Waterman
Pentagram, London

Wolfgang Hartmann
Fundación Tipografía Bauer, Barcelona

Walter R. Wybrands
BV Uitgeverij D Bataafsche Leeuw/Van Soeren & Co, Amsterdam

Neil Handley
British Optical Association Museum/The College of Optometrists, London

Michael Collinge, Oliver Clark
Collinge & Clark, London

Jan Tholenaar
The Jan Tholenaar Collection, Amsterdam

Brian Webb
Trickett & Webb, London

Thanks also to: Hiang Kee, Richard Hollis, Alan Fletcher, David Wakefield,
Jan Solpera, Misha Anikst, Alan E. Rapp, Janet Pilch, Marcela Ramirez,
Piers Wardle, John L.Walters, Stanislav Kolibal, Marqueta Kolibal, Jan de
Jong, Anne Clarke, Miranda Davies, Hilary Arnold.

EDITED BY JULIAN ROTHENSTEIN & MEL GOODING

# FEATURES

# INTRODUCTION

MEL GOODING

The letter, as an abstract written sign, developed from the pictogram, the simple drawing that accompanied speech into the making of the first human culture. The sign must exist, drawn by the finger in sand, marked in ash or ochre on the cave wall, scratched into clay by a stick, before the sound can be attached to it. "All letters began as signs" wrote Victor Hugo, "and all signs began as images." In a famous and not entirely fanciful little essay, the great novelist found in the modern alphabet everything from the image of man's simplest shelter to the portent of his destiny and the sign of God:

A is the roof, the gable with its crossbeam, the arch; or it is two friends greeting, who embrace and shake hands; D is the human back; B is the back on the back, the hump; C is the crescent, the moon; E is the foundations, the pillar, the console and the architrave, all architecture in a single letter; F is the gibbet; G is the french horn; H is a façade with two towers; I is the war machine launching its projectile; J is the ploughshare and the horn of plenty; K is the angle of reflection equal to the angle of incidence, a key to geometry; L is the leg and foot; M is a mountain or a camp with tents pitched in pairs; N is a gate with a diagonal bar; O is the sun; P is a porter with a load on his back; Q is a rump with a tail; R is the porter resting on his staff; S is a serpent; T is a hammer; U is the urn, V the vase, which are easily confused; (Y is a tree, a fork, the confluence of two rivers, a stemmed glass, a man with arms up-stretched); X is crossed swords, a battle: who will win we do not know, so the mystics made it the sign of destiny and the algebraists the sign of the unknown; Z is lightning, the sign of God: That is what the alphabet contains.

There is indeed something quite magical about the look of the alphabet: it has to do with its infinite capacity to change shape and style, to express purpose and suggest mood, to be formal and informal, elegant and ugly, classical and romantic, delicate and robust. Every alphabet presents an orchestration of the letters to the eye, is a kind of score, a systematic optical abstract, a visual matrix out of which any number of possible messages might be composed. This visual versatility is, of course, directly related to the uses to which letters are put, and the form and nature of any message will depend on the type and scale of the lettering.

In this book, for example, there is reproduced, for the first time since their publication, a series of sign-writers' alphabets intended to find their public realisation on shop fronts and bar signs; there are eye charts for the optician's patient; there are letters and signs for technical manuals; there is fine typography for beautiful books; there is a magisterial constructivist visual ballet; and so on. Every task demands its own kind of alphabet; every new purpose evolves its appropriate new lettering: of the making of alphabets there is no end.

We live in an age in which the use of letters, and recourse to diverse alphabets, is unprecedented, and in which more alphabets have been invented than ever before in history. In the period of modernism, whose progressive and humane principles we celebrate in this book, there was access as never before to good design and visual diversity. In magazines and books, on book jackets and film posters, in the packaging of goods and the advertisement of services, on buildings and in the streets, wherever information was conveyed there was evidence of the most intelligent and aesthetically sophisticated combination of utility and beauty.

The focus of this book, though not exclusively so, is on those alphabets, designs, and diverse printed materials of the modern era that embody the optimistic modernist spirit of the early and mid-twentieth century. Beyond that, it has no programme, and it makes no systematic presentation: it reflects the taste of the editors, their predilection for the wayward as well as for the rigorous in matters of design and typography. It is a book made for all lovers of letters and signs, for their use and for their delight.

# THE ALPHABET

GEORGES PEREC

I have several times asked myself what logic was applied in the distribution of the six vowels and twenty consonants of our alphabet. Why start with A, then B, then C, etc.?

The fact that there is obviously no answer to this question is initially reassuring: the order of the alphabet is arbitrary, impressive, and therefore neutral. Objectively speaking, A is no better than B, the ABC is not a sign of excellence but only of a beginning (the ABC of one's *métier*).

But the mere fact that there is an order no doubt means that, sooner or later and more or less, each element in the series becomes the insidious bearer of a qualitative coefficient. Thus a B movie will be thought of as "less good" than another film, which, as it happens, no one has yet thought of calling an "A movie." Just as a cigarette manufacturer who has the words "Class A" stamped on his packets is giving us to understand that his cigarettes are superior to others.

The qualitative alphabetical code is not very well stocked. In fact, it has hardly more than three elements:

A = excellent

B = less good

Z = hopeless

But this doesn't stop it being a code and superimposing a whole hierarchical system on a sequence that is by definition inert.

For reasons that are somewhat different but still germane to my purpose, it may be noted that numerous companies go out of their way in their corporate titles to end up with acronyms of the AAA, ABC, AAAc, etc. kind so as to figure among the first entries in professional directories and phone books. Conversely, a schoolboy does well to have a name whose initial letter comes in the middle of the alphabet because he will then stand a better chance of not being asked a question.

from *Penser/Classer* ("*Think/Classify*") translated by John Sturrock

*NOT*

The types are ~~arranged in~~
alphabetical order

# A

a

ABRICOT

APRICOT

APRIKOSE

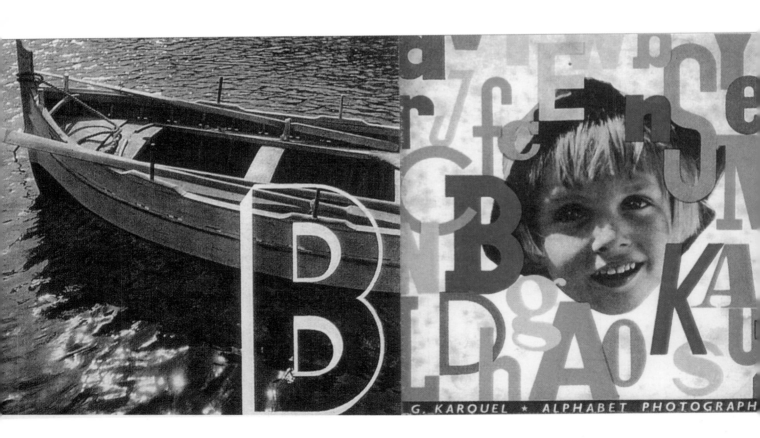

G. KARQUEL * ALPHABET PHOTOGRAPH

A B C D E F

G H J K L M

N O P Q R S

T U V X Y Z

SS

GB

SC

ET

BBS

MODÈLES DE

MW

FE

JEAN PUIFORCAT

SA

ME

L'AUTOMOBILE
ETOILE DE
L'INDUSTRIE FRANÇAISE

Tous les drapeaux du monde sont faits en soie de Lyon

le témoin.
DIRECTEUR PAUL IRIBE N 63 19 MAI 1935 LE N' UN FRANC
LA LOTERIE
A TOUS LES COUPS L'ON PERD

GAIETE SAGESSE Loyauté FRANÇAISES

# TIPPLER

Dusk to Dawn in the life of a Man-about-town, as shown by twenty-six different scenes, each decorating a letter of this tippler alphabet.

A B C D

E F G H I

J K L M

N O P Q R

S T U V

W X Y Z

TOME 1

TRAVAUX DE VILLE

ABCDEFG
HIJKLMN,
OPQRST.
UVWXYZ!
1234567890
abcdefgghij
klmnopqrst
uvwxyz.&?

त

तरबूज

श

थरमस

द

दवात

# ab

 bbcddeef
ghchrijkklmn
naoppgqrrss
otuvwwxgyyz

3039              3040              3041

# le mot.

N° 2. — 1re Année.　　　10 Centimes　　　Lundi 7 Déc. 1914.

**LOHENGRIN ET L'ÉCREVISSE**

DESSIN DE PAUL IRIBE

## LA MARCHE SUR PARIS.

# 144 Point
## Ludlow 6-EC Gothic Extra Condensed

ABCDEF

GHIJKLM

NOPQRST

UVWX

**NOTE**

For the remainder of this alphabet, points, figures, other characters, information, etc., see the following page

Y Z & 1 2 3 4

5 6 7 8 9 0 $

£ . : , - ' ? !

encres simili-creux

LEFRANC

LEFRANC

ROLAND
ANSIEAU

ABCDEFG

HIJKLŁM

NOPRST

U·W·Y·Z

·1234567890·

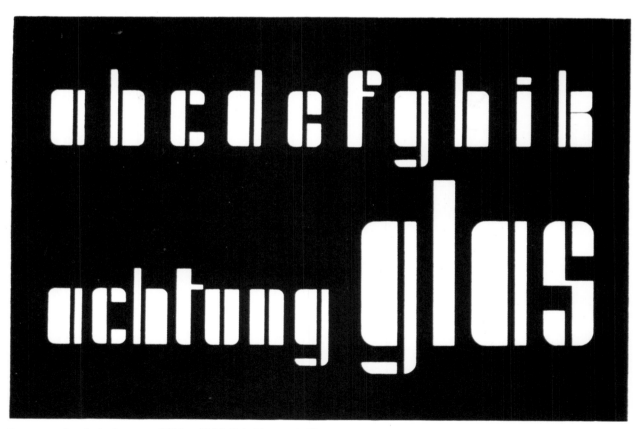

a b c d e f g h i j k
l m n o p q r s t
u v w x y z

Diese Schablonenschrift ist aus typographischem Material (Messinglinien) entstanden und kann, wie in den hier gezeigten Beispielen 1, 2, 3, systematisch breiter oder höher gemacht werden

a b c .₁    a b c .₂

a b c d e f g h i k

achtung glas

₃

Kunstgewerbeschule Stuttgart (Walter Veit). Schablonenschrift

KONSTRUIERTE SCHRIFTEN

1, Franz Stautner, Mannheim. Geschäftskarte der Buchdruckerei G. Jacob, Mannheim. 2, Grete Stern, Stuttgart. Cigaretten-packung. 3, Buchdruckerei C. Nypels, Maastricht. Plakat für eine Kunstausstellung. 4, Erich Matthes, Erasmus-Druck, Berlin. Anzeige für MK-Papier. 5, 7, Nicolai Ilijin, Nishnij-Nowgorod. Zwei Buchumschläge. 6, Unbek. Buchumschlag

TYPOGRAPHISCHE BEISPIELE

JAPANESE
OLD ORIENTAL
DINNERWARE
EXOTIC FISH
KIMONOS TIES
PAPER KITES

天回來他若今天不來呢那怎麼樣○有人說山西反了○這個事情

CHINESE
IS BEST
SEE LEFT
TO RIGHT,
BUT
VERTICAL
READING
IS QUITE
AUTHENTIC

ABCDEFGHH
IIJJKLLMNNO
中PPRSSTUV
WXYZ1234567890

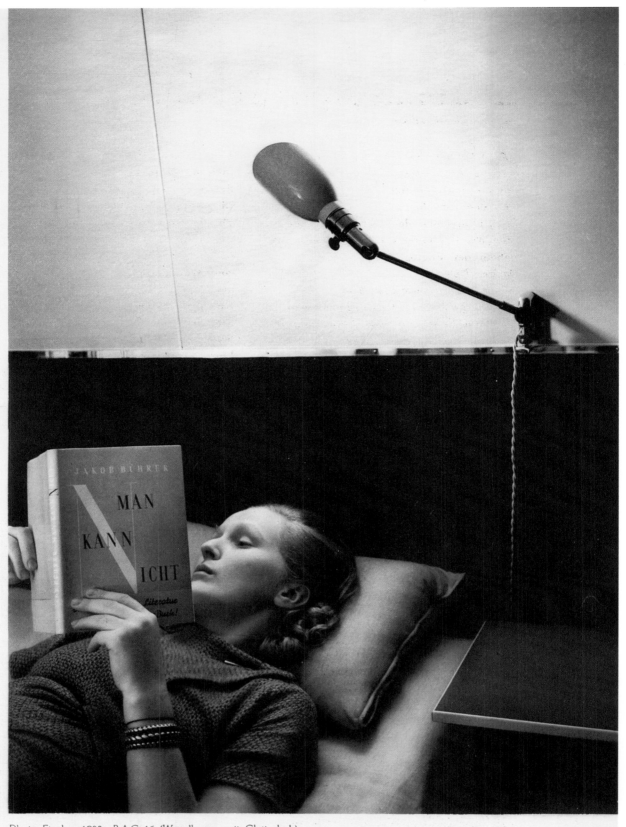

Photo Finsler, 1933: BAG 16 (Wandlampe mit Gleitschuh)

KUPFERTIEFDRUCK BÜCHLER & CO. BERN

ЖЕЛЕЗНОДОРОЖНИК ПОМНИ
БЕСПЕРЕБОЙНЫЕ ПЕРЕВОЗКИ ОСНОВА
УСПЕШНОГО ВЫПОЛНЕНИЯ ПЯТИЛЕТКИ
НАРОДНОГО ХОЗЯЙСТВА В ЧЕТЫРЕ ГОДА

Д.Буланов

ПЯТИЛЕТКА КАДРОВ ОБЩЕСТВЕННОГО ПИТАНИЯ

Заведующие столовыми и их заместителей 6600

ДИРЕКТОРОВ ФАБРИК КУХОНЬ И ИХ ЗАМЕСТИТЕЛЕЙ 957

ЭКОНОМИСТОВ, РАБОТН. Т.Н.Б. И СТАРШ. БУХГАЛТЕРОВ 1.298

ДИЭТЕТИКОВ ГИГИЕНИСТОВ 686

ИНЖЕНЕРОВ ХИМИКОВ 882 ИНЖЕНЕРОВ ТЕХНОЛОГОВ 882

КВАЛИФИЦИРОВАННЫХ 39.075 РАБОЧИХ ПОДРУЧНЫХ 53.985

ТЕХНИКОВ-МЕХАНИКОВ 1.285 ТЕХНИКОВ КУЛИНАРОВ 9.810

НАРПИТОВЕЦ ПОВЫШАЙ СВОЮ КВАЛИФИКАЦИЮ

# A CZECH MODERNIST ALPHABET

Karel Teige (1900-1951) was the greatest of the Czech avant-garde artist-writers of the 1920s and 1930s. His 1926 photomontage designs for the twenty-four-poem sequence *Abeceda*, written by his friend Víteslav Nezval, are a uniquely elegant and witty invention, one of the enduring achievements of Czech modernism. The designs feature the third collaborator in the project, the dancer Milca Mayarová, whose idea it was to choreograph the poems, creating a pose for each letter, and then to publish the book with Teige's title designs. Using Karel Paspa's photographs of Mayarová, which contrive to be both erotic and chastely gymnastic, Teige's designs transform the alphabet into what is effectively a constructivist manifesto, a demonstration of his aim to create a new "optical language, a system of signs capable of embodying words in graphic figures." It is a stunning realisation of what László Moholy-Nagy had called for in his influential 1925 Bauhaus book, *Painting, Photography, Film*, the dynamic combination of photographic image and lettering he termed "typofoto." Like Mayarová, Teige succeeds in finding an utterly original and distinctive solution for every letter: her brilliant pose alphabet is animated into a visual dance, what Nezval called "a living poem."

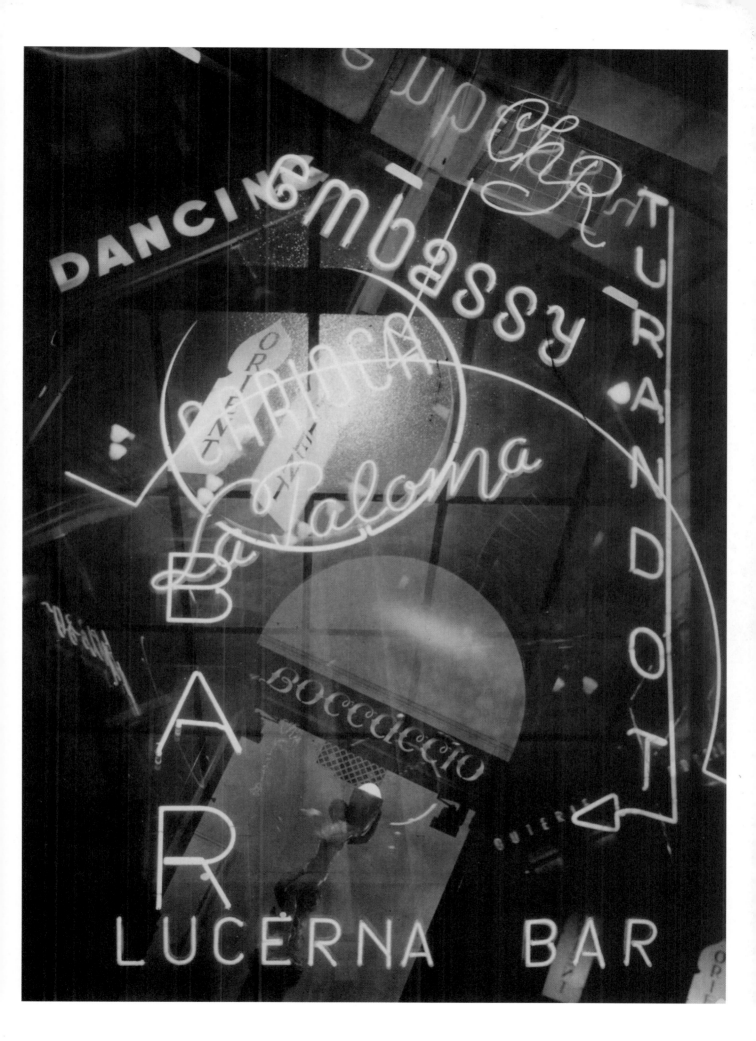

ABCDEF
GHIJKLM
NOPQRST
UVWXYZ

Rotterdamsche Schilderschool,
A. R. VAN DER BURG

A. R. VAN DER BURG.

ABCDEF
GHIJKLM
NOPQRST
UVWXYZ

Rotterdamsche Schilderschool,
A. R. VAN DER BURG.

A. R. VAN DER BURG.

a b c d e f g h i j
k l m n o p q r
s t u v w x y z
1 2 3 4 5 6 7 8 9 0

Rotterdamsche Schilderschool,
A. R. VAN DER BURG.

A. R. VAN DER BURG.

a b c d e f g h i
j k l m n o p q r
s t u v w x y z
1 2 3 4 5 6 7 8 9 0

Rotterdamsche Schilderschool,
A. R. VAN DER BURG

A. R. VAN DER BURG.

Publicité Dam.

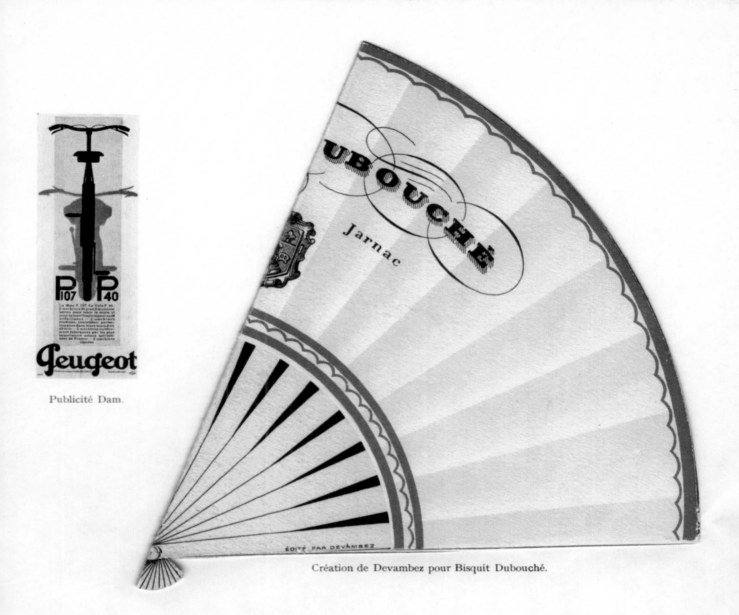

Création de Devambez pour Bisquit Dubouché.

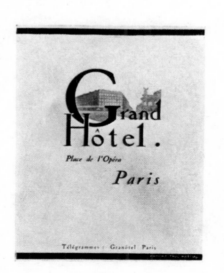

Annonce pour les montres Lip.

Page d'annonce (Édit. Paul-Martial).

Dessin de Francis Bernard
(Édit. Paul-Martial).

aaabcde

ghoqpsun

m ijrrlfftt!!..

xz vyw,;:

123456

67890

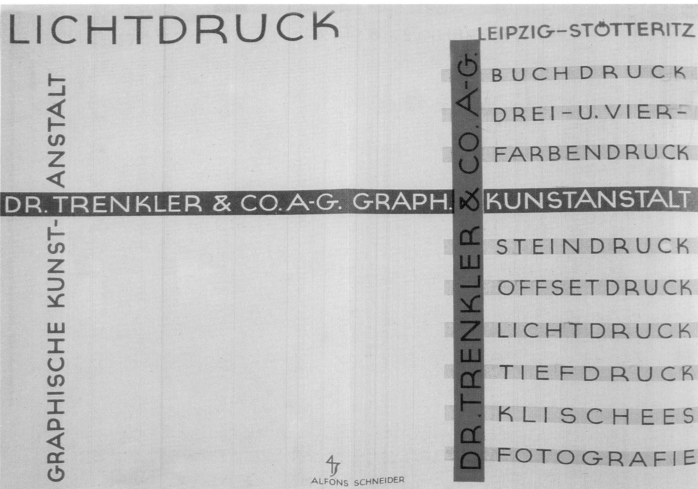

LICHTDRUCK

LEIPZIG–STÖTTERITZ

BUCHDRUCK

DREI–U. VIER–

FARBENDRUCK

GRAPHISCHE KUNST- ANSTALT

DR. TRENKLER & CO. A·G. GRAPH. KUNSTANSTALT

DR. TRENKLER & CO. A·G.

STEINDRUCK

OFFSETDRUCK

LICHTDRUCK

TIEFDRUCK

KLISCHEES

FOTOGRAFIE

ALFONS SCHNEIDER

ELEMENTARE
TYPOGRAPHIE
MIT
ERBAR
GROTESK
SCHRIFTEN
DER
SCHRIFTGIESSEREI
LUDWIG
&MAYER
FRANKFURT
AM MAIN

BEILAGE ZUR „GEBRAUCHSGRAPHIK"
ENTWURF, SATZ UND DRUCK
KÖLNER WERKSCHULEN
KLASSE ERBAR

Welche erfreuliche Veränderung zeigt sich schon seit zwei Jahrzehnten auf dem Gebiete der Schriftschneidekunst, gegenüber der Verflachung des Geschmackes in den letzten Jahrzehnten vorigen Jahrhunderts! Wir haben eine große Zahl von Antiquaschriften erhalten, die einen so hohen Grad der Durchgeistigung zeigen, daß sie den besten alten Vorbildern der Zeit des handwerklichen Schaffens an die Seite gestellt werden können.

Nur bei einer Schriftart, den Grotesk-Schriften, war seither von dem frischen Zug, der durch das Kunstgewerbe geht, nichts zu verspüren. Die Grotesk-Schriften hat man wohl in allen möglichen Breiten und Fetten gebracht, aber eine künstlerische Neugestaltung der Formen hat man unterlassen.

Man glaubte nach klassischen Vorbildern zu arbeiten und hat nur den Ungeschmack in eine verfeinerte Form gebracht, dadurch, daß man die langweilige Eintönigkeit noch peinlicher unterstrich.

EIN VIERTEL
JAHRHUNDERT
DRUCKFARBEN
FABRIKEN
GEBR.HARTMANN
HALLE-AMMENDORF

G. B. SHAW

Trakař jablek

Americký císař

G. B. SHAW

Člověk nikdy neví

G. B. SHAW

Drobnosti

Vzorný sluha Bashwille

Jak lhal jejímu manželu

Sutnar

G. B. Shaw

Drobnosti

Výstřižky z novin
Prohlédnutí Blanco Posneta

HÁNOSŮĚBL
JDCKMPRW
ČVXZYIFT

nahebydskr
ctmfjópžgvl
wx2345678u

abdeghk
npqc uu
mu dos
xyzfijrtl

ABCDEEF
GHIJKLM
NOPQRS
TUVVWX
YZ I.....CCC.

DIE
CENCI

DEUTSCHE
OPAK
GLAS
WERKE

abcdefghijklmno
pqrfstuvwxyz
ABCDEFGHIJKLMN
OPQRSTUVWXYZ

KONSTRUIERTE SCHRIFTEN

*Lettres majuscules.*

# ABCDE
# FGHIJK
# LMNOP
# QRSTU
# VWXYZ

ABCDEFG
HIJKLMN
OPQRST
UVWXYZ
abcdefghij
klmnopqrst
uvwxyzæœ

MILANO

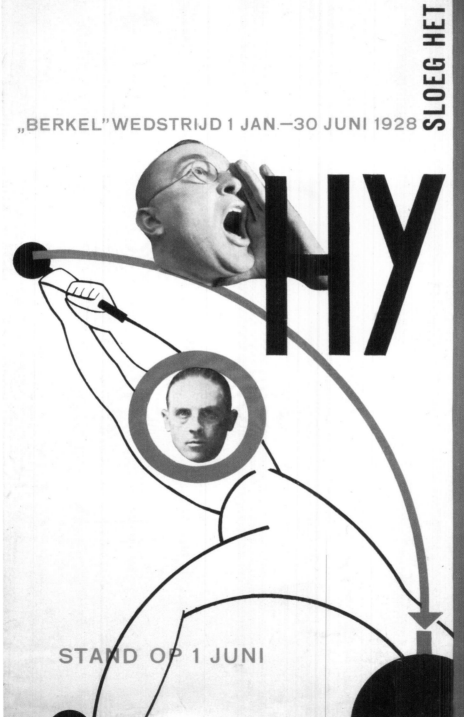

„BERKEL" WEDSTRIJD 1 JAN.—30 JUNI 1928

HY SLOEG HET HOOGST

| | |
|---|---|
| A. BOTERMANS Jr. | 141,3 % |
| J. C. KOOPMAN | 141,- % |
| E. ROMEIJN | 124,- % |
| D. DIJKSTRA | 121,9 % |
| W. LEGERSTEE | 121,6 % |
| G. DIEPENHEIM | 118,2 % |
| J. REBEL | 113,9 % |
| H. G. BOTERMANS | 110,3 % |
| H. HENNINK | 106,9 % |
| A. VAN VELZEN | 102,1 % |
| A. NOORDHOFF | 98,- % |
| M. DERKSEN | 96,6 % |
| A. BAMMENS | 94,7 % |
| C. VAN HOLST | 92,9 % |
| W. DE HAAS | 90,- % |
| F. GOOSEN | 87,5 % |
| H. J. F. KIECKENS | 82,3 % |
| D. VAN BELLE | 82,5 % |
| A. VOGEL | 80,1 % |
| D. VISSER | 73,7 % |
| H. VAN BOSSUM Sr. | 68,3 % |

STAND OP 1 JUNI

RECLAME PAUL SCHUITEM.

# ABCD
# EFGHI
# KLMN
# OPQR
# STUV
# WXYZ

XXᵉ SIECLE Nᵒ 4

XXᵗʰ CENTURY

ÉDITION IN ENGLISH

CHRISTMAS 1938

# THE ANTIFASCIST SCHOOLBOOK

In 1937 the republican government of Spain was deeply embroiled in the savage civil war against the fascist rebellion led by General Franco. Under the leadership of the minister of education, Jesús Hernández, the Ministry of Public Information issued *Cartilla Escolar Antifascista*, a literacy primer, as an aid to the campaign of the "cultural militias" against illiteracy. The booklet, beautifully designed by Mauricio Amster, who also created the poster advertising the "schoolbook", combined phonetics with politics, identifying the military struggle against fascism with the cultural fight against ignorance. Pages from this poignant document are reproduced here for the first time since its publication in republican Spain's heroic years of travail and hope. The civil war ended in March 1939, with the final defeat of the republic.

¡VIVA MADRID HEROICO!

VI-VA MA-DRID HE-ROI-CO

Vi-va Ma-drid he-roi-co

i, a, e, o

V, v, M, d, r, h, c

ejercicios: formar otras sílabas, palabras y frases con los elementos ya conocidos.

ejemplos de sílabas:

Ha, he, hi, ho, hu, re, mos, na, Es,
*Ha, he, hi, ho, hu, re, mos, na, Es,*

As, Is, Os, Us, pa, ña, ñe, fe, fa, fi,
*As, Is, Os, Us, pa, ña, ñe, fe, fa, fi,*

fo, fu, lir, lar, lur.
*fo, fu, lir, lar, lur.*

ejemplos de palabras:

Hacer, hago, haces, hacemos, hagamos, haréis, hacían,
*Hacer, hago, haces, hacemos, hagamos, haréis, hacían,*

hecho, haber, hiena, hierro, honda, hospital, huelga,
*hecho, haber, hiena, hierro, honda, hospital, huelga.*

Esteban, Ismael, fosa, fusil, feroz.
*Esteban, Ismael, fosa, fusil, feroz.*

## Nuestros combatientes luchan como
*Nuestros combatientes luchan como*

## héroes.
*héroes.*

# JESUS HERNANDEZ, NUESTRO MINISTRO DE INSTRUCCION

Je-sús Her-nán-dez, nues-tro
Mi-nis-tro de Ins-truc-ción.

J-e-s-ú-s H-e-r-n-á-n-d-e-z, n-u-e-s-t-r-o
M-i-n-i-s-t-r-o d-e I-n-s-t-r-u-c-c-i-ó-n.

i, e, u, a, o
J, s, H, r, n, d, z, M, I.

# SOLIDARIDAD INTERNACIONAL

So-li-da-ri-dad in-ter-na-cio-nal

o, i, a,

Tra, Tre, Tri, Tro, Tru, ba, be, je,
*Tra, Tre, Tri, Tro, Tru, ba, be, je,*

ja, ji, jo, ju, mos, mas, pa, pe, ra,
*ja, ji, jo, ju, mos, mas, pa, pe, ra,*

la, gue, gui, güe, güi, rra, rre.
*la, gue, gui, güe, güi, rra, rre.*

tropas, ultraje, jovial, agujero, jugo, racimo, ración,
*tropas, ultraje, jovial, agujero, jugo, racimo, ración,*

trinchera, Trubia, ametralladora, traje, ajetreo, trigo,
*trinchera, Trubia, ametralladora, traje, ajetreo, trigo,*

barra, rojo, jarra, jara, reloj, aparejo, guijarro,
*barra, rojo, jarra, jara, reloj, aparejo, guijarro*

pingüe, argüir.
*pingüe, argüir,*

## La juventud gloriosa se bate en
*La juventud gloriosa se bate en*

## las trincheras.
*las trincheras.*

REPUBLICA DEMOCRATICA

RE-PU-BLI-CA DE-MO-CRA-TI-CA

R-e-p-ú-b-l-i-c-a d-e-m-o-c-r-á-t-i-c-a

e, u, i, a, o

R, p, b, l, c, d, m, r, t

# LENIN, NUESTRO GRAN MAESTRO

Le-nin, nues-tro gran ma-es-tro

e, i, u, o, a

L, n, s, t, r, g, m

AÑO IV - NUMERO 3 (20)　　　　　　　　　MAYO - JUNIO 1953

# SIN◯SIS

REVISTA MEDICA

EDITADA POR "ESTABLECIMIENTOS MEXICANOS COLLIERE, S. A."

ATAVIOS DE LOS DIOSES.—*Códice matritense del Real Palacio.*

ARTE PREHISPANICO por *Vladimiro Rosado Ojeda,* pág. 19

EXPOSITION D'ART MEXICAIN
ANCIEN ET MODERNE

MUSEE NATIONAL D'ART MODERNE
PARIS · MAI-JUILLET 1952

MEXICO en el ARTE

número 12

· PALACIO DE BELLAS ARTES ·

OPeRa
NACIONAL
con la COLABORACION INBA
del
1951

# TRATAMIENTO DEL ALCOHOLISMO

## Etabus

Reg. No. 34480 S.S.A.    "LITERATURA EXCLUSIVA PARA MEDICOS    Prop. No. A-Fi- 8-5" aaaaa b bbbb c

dd e f g g h i j

k l m n o o o o p p

q q r r r ſ s t u v

w x x y z

А. Крученых

# ЕЖИПТИЕН

А Б В Г

Д Е Ж З И

К Л М Н О

П Р С Т У Ф Х

Ц Ч Ш Щ

Ъ Ь Ю Я

---

1 2 3 4 5 6 7

8 9 & 9 0

ABCDEFGHIJ
KĽMNOPQRS
ÓÍÝTUVXYZW !?

PRÍLOHA 1
*Pražský grotesk*

АБВГГДЕДЖЗИЙК
ЛЛМНОПРСТУФХ
ЦЧШЩЩЭЮЯЯЁЬЫЬЪ

PRÍLOHA 2
*Azbuka úzka*

CAPRONI «1»

27 MAGGIO 1910

CAPRONI
NELLA GRAN
DE GUERRA
1915-18 CAPRO
NI "450" PER LA
RICONQUISTA
DELLA LIBIA
CAPRONI "74"
CAPRONI "114 A.Q.

PRIMATI MONDIALI DI ALTEZZA CAPRONI IN
ETIOPIA CAPRONI "M. RICOGNIZIONE CAPRO
NI "101" BOMBARDAMENTO LEGGERO "133 BOM
BARDAMENTO PESANTE CAPRONI IN SPAGNA

AEROPLANI

ABCDEFI
GHJKLM
NOPQRW
STUVYXZ

abcdefg
hijklno
mpqrfw
stuvxyz

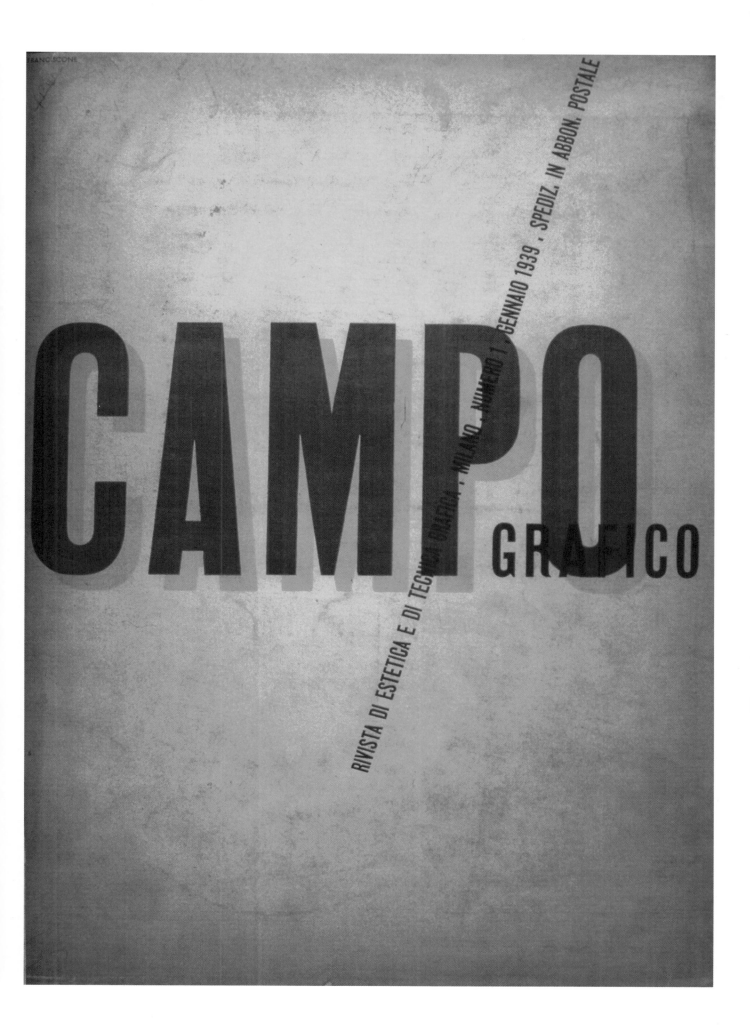

# CAMPO GRAFICO

RIVISTA DI ESTETICA E DI TECNICA GRAFICA · MILANO · NUMERO 1 · GENNAIO 1939 · SPEDIZ. IN ABBON. POSTALE

ABCDE
FGHIJK
LMNOP
QRSTU
VWXYZ
&$!?&&
12345
67890

ИЛЬЯ ЗДАНЕВИЧ

зохна и женихи

# le mot.

N° 17. — 1ʳᵉ Année.        30 Centimes.        Samedi 1ᵉʳ Mai 1915.

DESSIN DE PAUL IRIBE.

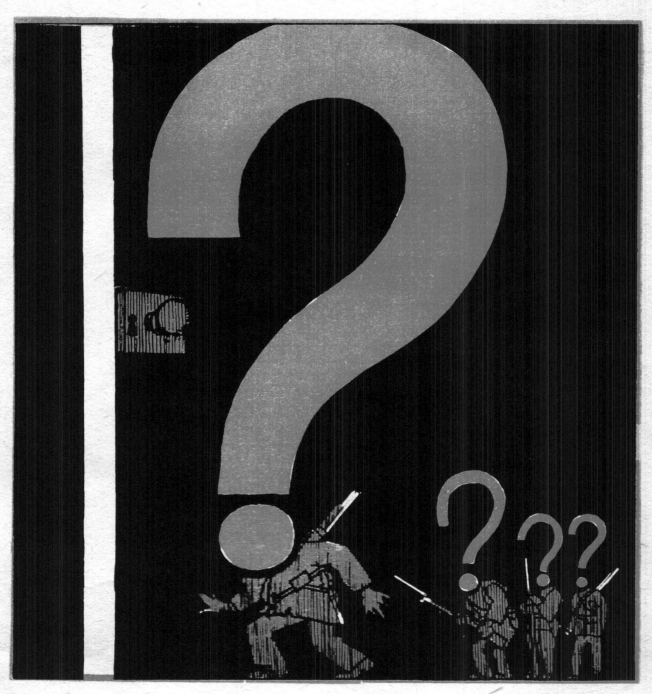

LA VEILLÉE DES NEUTRES.

HNBDICRMKE
GOPÁVSYŮWL
JŠTZXFMYJQ

1234567890 2

abrphxfcvdn.
stgmjúyeikz

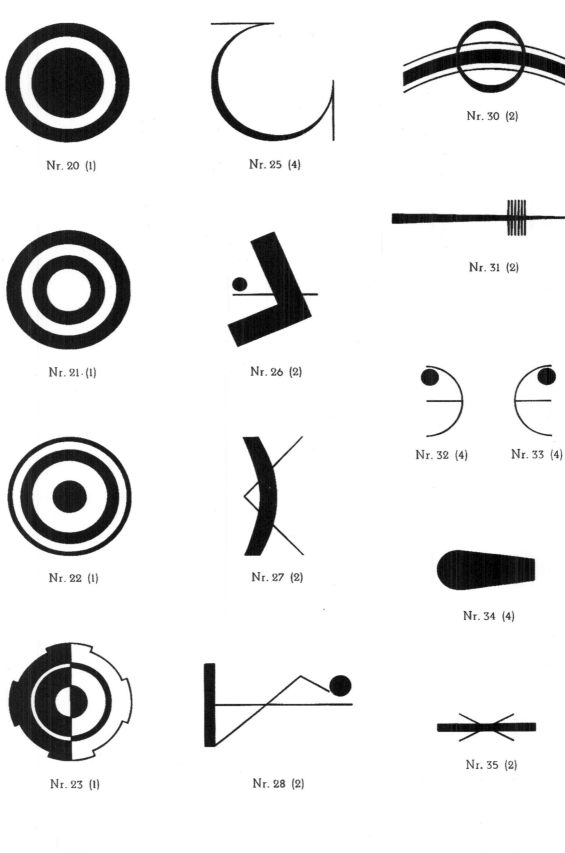

Nr. 20 (1)

Nr. 25 (4)

Nr. 30 (2)

Nr. 21 (1)

Nr. 26 (2)

Nr. 31 (2)

Nr. 22 (1)

Nr. 27 (2)

Nr. 32 (4)     Nr. 33 (4)

Nr. 34 (4)

Nr. 23 (1)

Nr. 28 (2)

Nr. 35 (2)

Nr. 24 (2)

Nr. 29 (2)

Nr. 36     Nr. 37     Nr. 38

Einfassung 1 m

abcdefghijk

œlmnopqrstuy

wxz

xyz

*Crous-Vidal, dont l'exposition à la Galerie d'Orsay fut le "clou" graphique de la rentrée 52, a dédié à Jean Giono et à l'école de Lure ce flamboyant caractère d'inspiration méditerranénne :*
*LES CATALANES*

LES CATALANES

ISCANRD123

FGHJKLMOPTUV

# TWO SIMPLE STEPS TO STENCIL MARKING

## 1
### CUT THE STENCIL

## 2
### MARK THE SHIPMENT

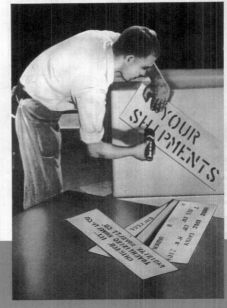

Slip in a sheet of stencil board—turn the wheel—press the handle. In a minute or less you have cut a stencil—clean, accurate.

Operators soon learn to cut stencils on the Marsh Machine with lighting speed because of the improved features shown on pages 20 and 21.

Lay the stencil on the shipment—make a few strokes with the Marsh Fountain Brush and you have a stencil mark—water-proof, smear-proof, permanent.

Marsh Inks made in black and various colors for marking boxes, cartons, metal, all kinds of shipments are shown on pages 26 to 29.

6

7

No. 1 Office, Shipping Dept. Assembly Dept.
No. 2 Machine Shop, Ink Dept. Oil Board Dept.
No. 3 Warehouse, Raw Material Storage.

**J. W. MARSH**
1869—1935
Founder

**WALT MARSH**
President

**E. J. MARSH**
Sec'y & Treas.

**PAUL WAGNER**
Ass't Treas. & Legal Counsel

**HERBERT W. HEMPEL**
Chief Engineer

**FRED BUCHMANN**
Plant Supt.

MOST men set out to make their mark in the world. Marsh of Belleville was different. He set out to help other men make their marks.

Yes, the most legible marks of all—STENCIL MARKS. Neat, bold, attractive, permanent. Marks that say: "This shipment is from a firm that's proud of its product, service, reputation."

From the Marsh Factory flow the stencil machines, brushes, inks, stencil board to serve industry and transportation, to aid business—free enterprise—in its task of serving all the people.

## MARSH STENCIL MACHINE COMPANY
### BELLEVILLE, ILLINOIS, U. S. A.

| U. S. AGENCIES | DENVER | MINNEAPOLIS | ST. LOUIS | FOREIGN AGENCIES | INDIA |
|---|---|---|---|---|---|
| ATLANTA | DETROIT | NASHVILLE | ST. PAUL | ARGENTINA | MEXICO |
| BALTIMORE | DULUTH | NEW HAVEN | SALT LAKE | AUSTRALIA | NETHERLANDS |
| BIRMINGHAM | EL PASO | NEW ORLEANS | SAN ANTONIO | BELGIUM | NEWFOUNDLAND |
| BOISE | FORT WORTH | NEW YORK CITY | SAN FRANCISCO | BRAZIL | NORWAY |
| BOSTON | HARTFORD | OMAHA | SEATTLE | CANADA | PHILIPPINE ISLANDS |
| BRIDGEPORT | HOUSTON | PHILADELPHIA | SPOKANE | CHILE | POSTO RICO |
| BUFFALO | KANSAS CITY | PHOENIX | SYRACUSE | COLOMBIA | SWEDEN |
| CHICAGO | LOS ANGELES | PITTSBURGH | TACOMA | CUBA | SWITZERLAND |
| CINCINNATI | LOUISVILLE | PORTLAND | TAMPA | ENGLAND | URUGUAY |
| CLEVELAND | MEMPHIS | PROVIDENCE | TOLEDO | FRANCE | UNION OF S. AFRICA |
| DALLAS | MILWAUKEE | ROCHESTER | WASHINGTON, D. C. | HAWAII | VENEZUELA |

**REPUTATION FOR LEADERSHIP IS EARNED BY YEARS OF TRUSTWORTHY PERFORMANCE**

One bank of drilling spindles

Dies finished for perfect accuracy

Quality Control Inspection

Making Stencil Ink—Black & Colors

Turning Die Carriers to size

Assembling the Marsh Fountain Brush

Presses for high-speed production

Assembling Marsh Stencil Machines

Group of skilled Punch Fitters

Final Inspection and Approval

Sales Dept. expedites orders

On their way to serve and save

This is an actual reproduction of the stencil characters cut by Model S (¾″ size) Marsh Stencil Machine.

Model S ¾″ Machine cuts this size stencil, one to four lines, any length. For marking medium sized shipments. Size of Machine 21″ x 16″ x 10″ high. Weight 100 lbs. Packed 145 lbs.

**Size of Stencil Board for Model S ¾″ Machine**

1-line 3″ x 20″
2-line 4″ x 20″
3-line 5″ x 20″
4-line 6″ x 20″

**¾″**

ABCDEFGHIJ
KLMNOPQRST
UVWXYZ' /&,
23456789-.

**This is an actual reproduction of the stencil characters cut by the Model R (1″ size) Marsh Stencil Machine.**

Model R 1″ Machine cuts this size, one to four lines, any length. For marking large shipments. Size of machine 24″ x 18″ x 10″ high. Weight 145 lbs. Packed 195 lbs.

**Size of Stencil Board for Model R 1″ Machine.**

1-line 4″ x 20″ or 24″     3-line 6″ x 20″ or 24″
2-line 5″ x 20″ or 24″     4-line 7″ x 20″ or 24″

**1″**

ABCDEFGHIJ
KLMNOPQRST
UVWXYZ' /&,
23456789-.

*i i i i u n m r c a o e v w x z ž s j*

*y q g p l t d b h ch k f*

*IHLFETJUCGOQXYVWŽŻ*

*I. II. V. X.*     *AMNDPBRKS*     *L.C.D.M.*

*1 2 3 4 5 6 7 8 9 0.*

*Achilles, Tantalus, Palermo, Vesuv.*

ABČCDEFGHIJKLMNOPQR
ŘSŠTUVWXYZŽ&
abcdefghijklmnopqrstuvwxyz
1234567890 I. II. III. IV. V. VI. VII. VIII. IX. X.

ABČCDEFGHIJKLMNOP
QRŘSŠTUVWXYZŽ&
abcdefghijklmnopqrstuvxyz
1234567890 I. II. III. IV. V. VI. VII. VIII. IX. X.

OT. ŠTORCH-MARIEN

KILIMA-
NDŽARO
LÁSKY

# Nr. 2

WERBEWESEN:

## DAS SCHAUFENSTER

## „Sie können ruhig Ihren Mittagsschlaf sich gönnen!"

Organisieren Sie Ihre Werbetätigkeit! Die arbeitet für Sie und trägt Gewinn herein, auch wenn Sie schlafen.

**Flugblätter mit dem Buntquadrat** werden herausgegeben von Max Burchartz. Sie erscheinen bei der Westdeutschen Treuhandgesellschaft Canis & Co., K.-G., Bochum. Sie bringen Aufsätze (meist mit Abbildungen) von Künstlern und Fachleuten über allgemeine und besondere Fragen der Kultur und Organisation, der Baugestaltung, der Formgestaltung von Industrieerzeugnissen und über Werbewesen.

Bewahren Sie jedes „Flugblatt mit einem Buntquadrat" gut auf! Sehen Sie ab u. zu hinein! Es bringt Ihnen Gewinn, sofern Sie seine Ratschläge befolgen.

ABCDEFGHIJ
KLMNOPQR
STUVWXYZ

abcdefghijklm
nopqrstuvwxyz

**werbe-
entwurf**
und ausführung

**dessau,bauhaus
d**

**herbert-bayer
b**

das wesen einer aufgabe muß erforscht und erkannt werden, dann wird die äußere erscheinung einer werbsache das logische mittel sein zum zweck, den die werbsache erfüllen soll.      eine arbeit nach dieser auffassung verbürgt überzeugungskraft und qualität.          alle darstellungsmittel der typografie, fotografie, malerei, zeichnung . . . . . wenden sich zweckmäßig an bei:                warenzeichen, geschäftspapier, inserat, prospekt, plakat, packung, werbebau und anderen werbsachen. seine fachlichen kenntnisse und erfahrungen sichern eine wirtschaft-

vdr-kartei
werbindust
februar 19

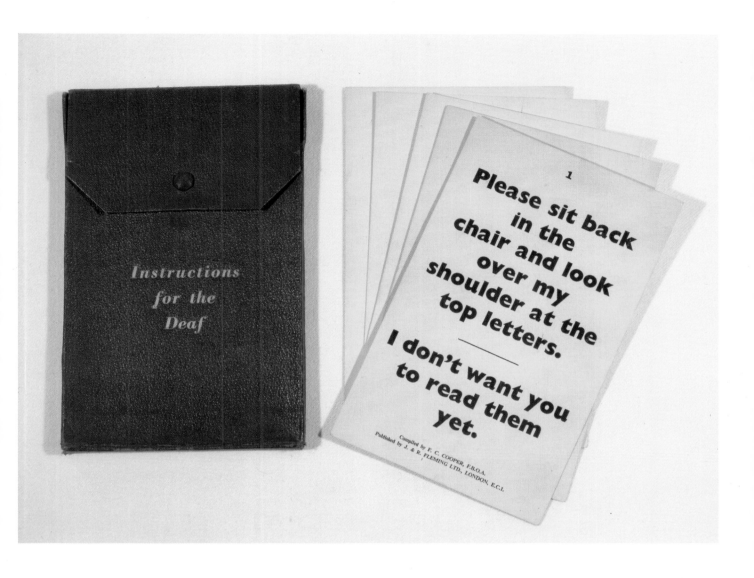

The photograph shows a dark booklet cover reading "*Instructions for the Deaf*" beside a set of cards, the top card reading:

1

**Please sit back in the chair and look over my shoulder at the top letters.**

**I don't want you to read them yet.**

Compiled by F. C. COOPER, F.B.O.A.
Published by J. & R. FLEMING LTD., LONDON, E.C.I.

# EYE TEST CHARTS

Eye test charts using letters of the alphabet, designed to test visual acuity and the efficacy of corrective lenses, were introduced in the 1830s. To increase optical distance in the testing room, some charts are designed with reversed letters and viewed through a facing mirror. In 1862 the Utrecht optometrist Herman Snellen designed the first scientifically reliable charts for testing vision distance, using carefully size-adjusted letters based on the typeface "Egyptian Paragon". Sans-serif letters, having less visual distraction, were introduced soon after. (Gill Sans Bold has been especially popular with British opticians.) In the 1870s Snellen introduced charts with calibrated lines and abstract figures for young or illiterate patients. Eye test chart designs all over the world are still based on Snellen's pioneering "Optotypes". The economy and clarity demanded by its function gave the eye test chart a typographic formal elegance that was modernist *avant la lettre.*

ARTS ET METIERS GRAPHIQUES

LETTRES

18 RUE SEGUIER PARIS 6

# FREGIO MECANO

### (Carattere scomponibile)

Minimo Kg. 2,50

Si vendono anche figure separate : minimo Kg. 1 per figura

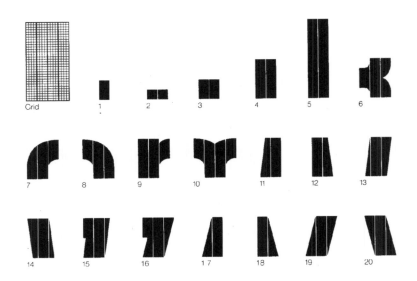

Crid 1 2 3 4 5 6

7 8 9 10 11 12 13

14 15 16 17 18 19 20

abcdefghijk

lmnopqrſstu

uʋxyz

This type is set with typographical material (Brass Rule). The letter ‹a› below shows how the individual pieces are assembled.

aaaaaaß

graphische abteilung der

rüürttembergischen

staatlichen

A specimen showing the possibilities in letter formation

kunstgeruerbeschule stuttgart

School of decorative Art, Stuttgart. Brass Rule Letters

CONSTRUCTED LETTERS

AA B CC DD
EE FF G HH
I J K LL M
NN O PP Q
RR SS TT UU
V W X Y Z
Æ Œ Ç & Cie
( ) . , ; : ' - (( )) ! ?
1 2 3 4 5 6 7 8 9 0

JUGEZ LA VALEUR DE NOS SERVICES PAR DEUX FAITS PRÉCIS

EDITIONS PAUL·MARTIAL PARIS

**MAQUETTES** **DEVIS**
PREPARÉS GRATUITEMENT

AFFICHES

CATALOGUES

DÉPLIANTS

INK SPOTS

B 12

PER FONT $1 25

abcdefghij

klmnopqrs

tuvwxyz

1234567890

ARTS ET MÉTIERS GRAPHIQUES

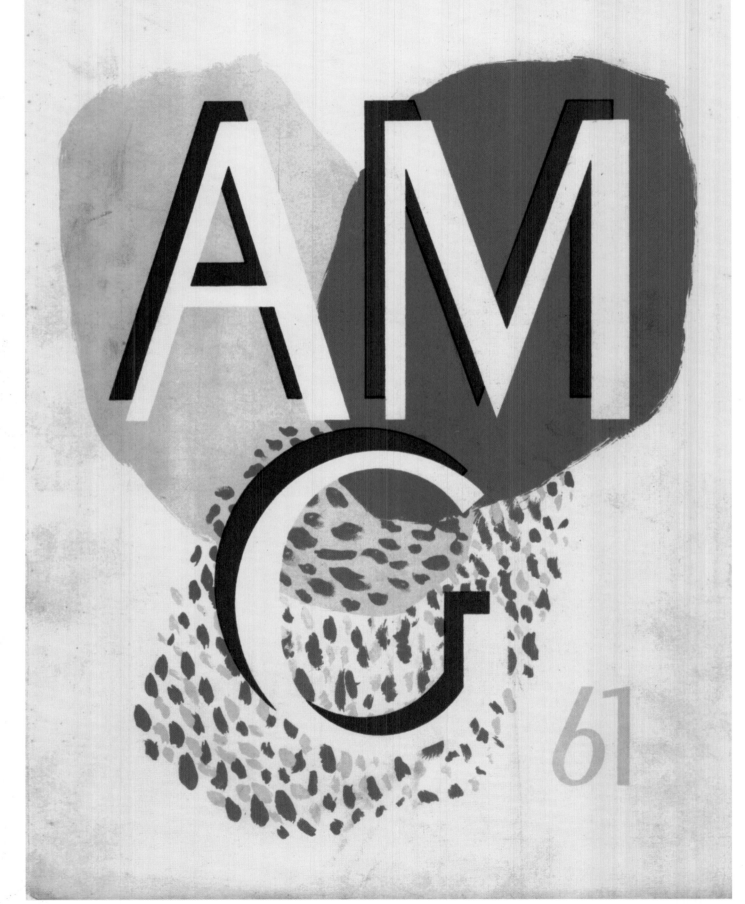

ARTS ET MÉTIERS GRAPHIQUES

# A B C D E F
# G H I J K L M
# N O P Q R S T
# U V W X Y Z

Rotterdamsche Schilderschool,
A. R. VAN DER BURG.

A. R. VAN DER BURG.

# a b c d e f g h i
# j k l m n o p q r s
# t u v w x i j y z
# 1 2 3 4 5 6 7 8 9 0

Rotterdamsche Schilderschool,
A. R. VAN DER BURG.

A. R. VAN DER BURG.

ĀBCDEFGHI
JKLMNŌPQ
RSTŪVWXY
ZI234
567890

HNBDIČRMKÉ
GOPAVSYUWL
JSTZXFMYJQ!,

1234567890:
abrphxfcvdn,
stgmjuyeikz

# КЛАСИЦИСТИЧНА АНТИКВА

АБВГДЕ

ЖЗИЙКЛМ

НОПРСТУ

ФХЦЧШЩ

ЪЬЮЯ

1234567890

A B C D E
F G H I J
K L M N O
P Q R S T
U V X Y Z

ABCDEFGHI
JKLMNOPQ
RSTUVWXYZ

ABCDEFGHJ
KLMNOPQR
STUVXYZ

ABCDEFGHIJ

KLMNOPQRS

TUVXYZ

A D E G H J K

M N O R S Y Z

1 2 3 4 5 6 7 8 9

abcdefghij
klmnopqrs
tuvwxyz

abcdef
ghijklm
nopqrs
tuvxyz
1234567890.&

O 74

COMPAGNONS DE COCAGNE

MENU POTAGE VELOUTÉ CAROLINE • ENDIVES AU JUS

DU 12 NOVEMBRE

CHEZ VINCENT CANDRÉ RUE SAINT ANDRÉ DES ARCS

TURBOT DE DIEPPE AU BEURRE D'ISIGNY • PERDREAUX BONNE FEMME

POMMES BONNE FEMME

CORBEILLE DE FRUITS

COQ A LA BERRICHONNE

HARICOTS VERTS

SALADE PANACHÉE FROMAGES FLANQUÉS D'ALOUETTES

VIN ROSÉ DE BOLÈNE

VIN BLANC DE POUILLY-SUR-LOIRE

PINOT DU SANCERROIS

CHAVIGNOLE

CAFÉ FINE ET ARMAGNAC

Menu du XVIᵉ dîner des Compagnons de Cocagne

MARMITE M NORMANDE. TURBAN ACON
D'ANGUILLE AU CHA- BLANC
BLIS. SELLE DE VEAU FAR- EN CA-
CIE ORLOFF AVEC UNE GAR- RAFE.
NITURE PRINTANIÉRE. ASPER- FLEUR
GES DE VINEUIL SAUCE HOL- IE EN PI-
LANDAISE. CŒUR DE ROMAI- CHET.
NE A L'HUILE D'OLIVE. FRO- GEVREY
MAGES. FRAISES CHAN- CHAM-
TILLY. CORBEILLE BERTIN
DE FRUITS. CAFÉ. E A U X-
DE-VIE DU PAYS

166

ABCDEFG
HIJKLMN
OPQRSTU
VWXYZ&!

abcdefghijklmn

opqrstuvwxyz!

123456789

A B C D E F G H I J K L M N O P Q R
S T U V W X Y Z ★ 1 2 3 4 5 6 7 8 9 ★ ?

a b c d e f g h i j k l m
n o p q r s t u v w x y z

VARIETY
•
VARIETY

– it's the RESULT that COUNTS !

A B C D E F G H I J K L
M N O P Q R S T U V W X
Y Z 1 2 3 4 5 6 7 8 9 ?

VARIETY

A B C D E F G H I J K L
M N O P Q R S T U V W
X Y Z 1 2 3 4 5 6 7 8 9

VARIETY

Ever Ready LABELS GO PLACES and DO THINGS

528 IDEAS for AMERICAN BUSINESS

Save Time    Save Money    Speed Production

ᑌᑌᑌᑌᑌᑌᑌᑌᐰᗷᗷ
ᑕᑕᑕᗪᗪᗪᕮᕮᕮᖴᖴᖴ
ᑕᑕᕼᕼᕼᕮᒍᒍᒍᛕᛕᛕ
ᒪᒪᒪᒪᗰᗰᗰᗰᛁᐰᐰᐰ
ᐰᐰOOOᑭᑭᑫᑫᖇᖇᔕ
ᔕᔢᔢᔢᑌᑌᑌᑌᑌᐯᐯᐯ
ᑌᒍᗯᗯ᙭᙭ᖾᖾᘔ&
1234567891O
(.,:,"!§?';-)

ČTYŘCICERO „PATRONA" GROTESK RUSKÉ

А Б В Г Д Е Ж З И І
А БВ VU ГО ДД Е ЖŽ ZZ ИI I

Й К Л М Н О П Р С
ЙJ К ЛL М НN О ПР PR CS

Т У Ф Х Ц Ч Ш Щ Ъ
Т УU ФF ХCH ЦС ЧČ ШŠ ЩŠČ Ъ

Ы Ь Ѣ Э Ю Я Ѳ Ѵ
ЫY Ь ѢĚ ЭE ЮJU ЯJA ѲF ѴI neb Y

Љ Њ Ћ Ђ Ј Џ Ж Ж
ЉLJ ЊŇ ЋT ЂĎ ЈJ ЏDŽ ЖA ЖJA

В.А. ФРАНЦЕВЪ
ПРАГА

171

A B C D E F G H I

J K L M N Ñ O P Q

R S T U V W X Y Z

Æ . , ; : Œ

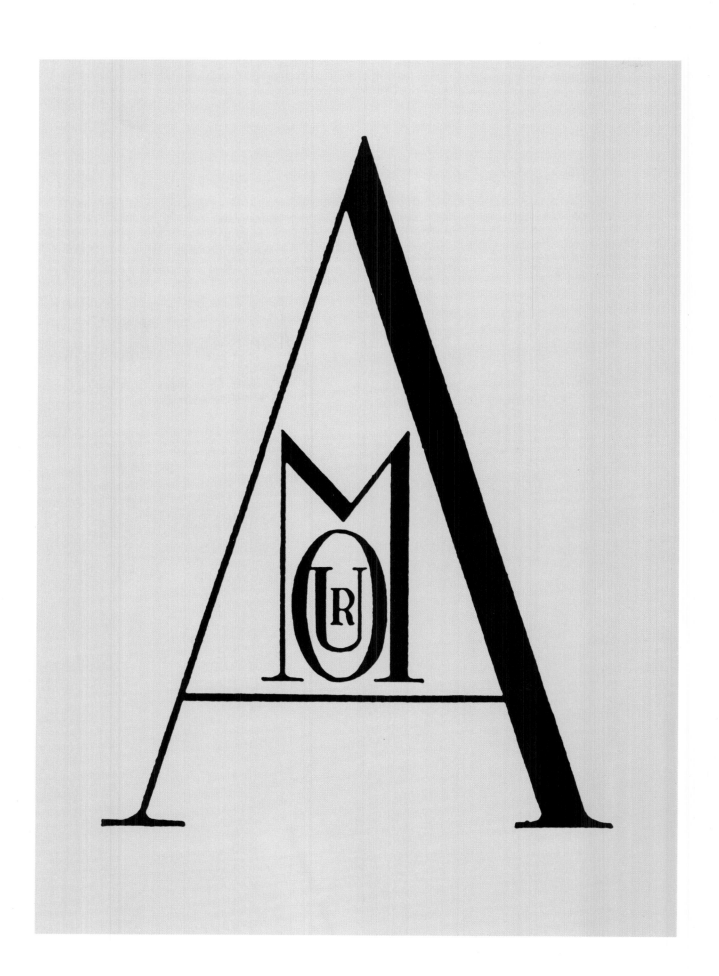

abcdefghikl

moprstuvw

xyz

A B C

D E F G H

I J K L M

N O P Q R

S T U V W

X Y Z

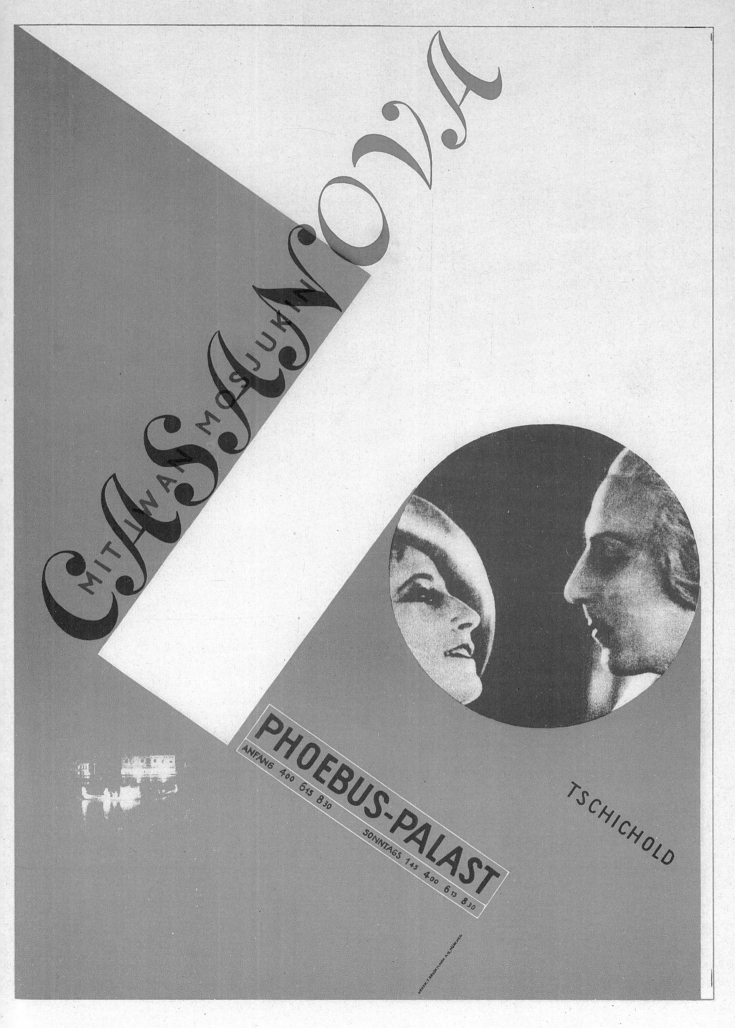

CASANOVA

MIT IWAN MOSJUKIN

PHOEBUS-PALAST

ANFANG 4.00 6.15 8.30

SONNTAGS 1.45 4.00 6.15 8.30

TSCHICHOLD

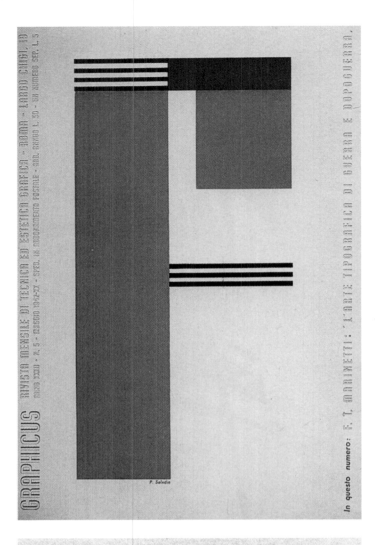

GRAPHICUS RIVISTA MENSILE DI TECNICA ED ESTETICA GRAFICA - ROMA - LARGO CHIGI, 19 - ANNO XXIII - N. 5 - GIUGNO 1942-XX - SPED. IN ABBONAMENTO POSTALE - GR. BANCO L. 30 - UN NUMERO SEP. L. 5

In questo numero: F. T. MARINETTI: L'ARTE TIPOGRAFICA DI GUERRA E DOPOGUERRA.

P. Saladin

CAMPO GRAFICO
AEROPORTO DELLA
RIVOLUZIONE
FUTURISTA DEL·
LE PAROLE IN LI
BERTA POESIA
PUBBLICITARIA

*tipografia velocità simultaneità*

*F. T. Marinetti*

MARINETTI
MARINETTI
MARINETTI
MARINETTI
MARINETTI
MARINETTI
MARINETTI
MARINETTI

# L'ITALIA FUTURISTA

DIREZIONE ARTISTICA
BRUNO CORRA · E. SETTIMELLI

E morto UMBERTO BOCCIONI caro grande forte migliore divino genio futurista ieri denigrato oggi glorificato superarlo superarlo superarlo durezza eroismo velocità avanti giovani futuristi tutto tutto doloresanguevita per la grande Italia sgombra ingigantita agilissima elettrica esplosiva non lagrime acciaio acciaio!

MARINETTI

IL PUGNO ITALIANO DI BOCCIONI

*DISEGNO DI BALLA FUTURISTA*

A Parigi, a Monaco, a Berlino, ovunque si parlasse male dell'Italia fuori d'Italia, Boccioni con la sua violenza e col suo ingegno si batteva coraggiosamente.

Ecco perchè volevano la guerra, egli e i suoi amici, quando nessuno la pensava, perchè sapevano quanto ingiusta fosse la svalutazione delle forze nazionali e quante oscure potenti radici avrebbero germogliato il giorno che la coscienza delle proprie forze le avesse nutrite.

178

ABCDEFGHIJ
KLMNOPQRS
TUVWXYZ$!?
1234567890

ABCDEFGHIJKL
MNOPQRSTUV
WXYZ&.,-':,!?
$1234567890

EL

MEP

MA

BJ

DT

SJ

MODÈLES DE

BC

JEAN PUIFORCAT

SE

AP

# KONSTRUKTIVISMUS
## IN THEORIE UND PRAXIS

Ein Gespräch ● Sprecher **A** ein erster Akzidenzer, **B** ein Bachulke ● Kollege **B** spinnt: Na, da habt'r ja wieder was Schönes eingerührt! **A** Ach, Sie meinen wohl die „elementare typographie"? **B** Nu freilich, man spricht doch heute nur noch von der „neuen Kunst"—?—Da muss ich gleich lachen! Der alte Gutenberg wird sich im Grabe rumdrehen über solche Kunst! **A** Haben Sie denn nicht seinerzeit in dem TM-Heft gelesen, dass die Konstruktivisten den Krieg an alle „Kunst" erklärt haben? **B** Nee, was da alles geschrieben wurde, ist mir viel zu hoch. Das kann so'n simpler alter Knabe wie ich nicht mehr verdauen. - Aber ihr Jungen, ihr seid ja helle! **A** Ich muss auch sagen, dass die Häufung von gleichbedeutenden Fremdwörtern das Verständnis der Sache nur erschwert, und es wäre besser gewesen, die Artikel mehr für den Laien gedacht zu schreiben. **B** Ja, sie müssten „elementarer" sein! **A** Nun aber die Beispiele, was meinen Sie dazu? **B** So 'ne Frage! Lächerlich, verrückt natürlich. Wenn sich das früher einer gewagt hätte, wäre er zum Tempel raus geflogen. **A** Das haben Sie bisher immer gesagt, wenn etwas Neues kam, und dann hat man sich daran gewöhnt, ja selber mitgemacht. **B** Davon kann hier keine Rede sein. Das geht jedem Buchdrucker von Fleisch und Blut gegen den Strich. Gequirlter Satz und Fischhaufen gehören abgelegt, aber nicht gedruckt! **A** Ach, das bezieht sich wohl auf Seite 196 und 201 des TM-Heftes? Ja, es gibt eben bei jeder Sache Übergriffe, und dann ist ja das ganze Thema Konstruktivismus erst ein Weg, noch kein Ziel. **B** Besser gesagt, es ist alles noch

SIGNET DER ORTSGRUPPE DRESDEN
ENTWURF WALTHER KÖNIG DRESDEN

unreif. Na, das sieht man ja auch! **A** Sie dürfen das nicht so verallgemeinern, lieber Kollege. Entschieden sind Beispiele zu sehen, denen man ihre Berechtigung nicht absprechen kann, die in ihrer betonten Einfachheit und Sachlichkeit eine gute Wirkung haben. **B** Und die Kolumnenziffer, he? Ist das auch Einfachheit, Sachlichkeit, wenn man sie erst suchen muss? **A** Die Konstruktivisten sind bestrebt, alles anders zu machen, wie bisher. Und so haben sie einmal etwas anderes versucht, was eben nicht allen gefällt und doch mit der rhythmischen Aufteilung einer Fläche begründet ist. **B** Nu, da macht eben jeder nach seinem Stiefel, was ihm gerade einfällt. Vielleicht stellt er mal eine Seite auf den Kopf, die nächste quer— was wollt ihr denn — er arbeitet doch „konstruktivistisch"! Wer lacht da? **A** Es ist nicht hübsch von Ihnen, Kollege, die Sache ins Lächerliche zu ziehen. So einfach, wie es aussieht, ist es nun doch nicht. Mit viel Bedacht und nicht willkürlich sind die Zeilen angeordnet und die Flächen verteilt. Machen Sie doch den Versuch und füllen Sie eine weisse Fläche mit verschieden gearteten und geformten Elementen, die Sie sich vielleicht aus schwarzem Papier schneiden, und Sie werden die Schwierigkeit erkennen, die sich ergibt, wenn man etwas organisch gestalten will. **B** Was hat denn diese Spielerei mit uns zu tun? Wir machen das, was man uns sagt, und haben uns im übrigen den Wünschen und Angaben der Kunden zu fügen, und die werden sich für solche tote Klötzer-Manier bestens bedanken. **A** Einfachheit kann man nicht als tot bezeichnen, und ich versichere Ihnen, dass es

BRIEFKOPF-ENTWURF

ALEXANDER MATHEJA DRESDEN

## WALTHER GLÖCKNER

Betracht, und so wird auch für die elementare Typographie meist die Groteskschrift verwendet, weil sie das Ursprüngliche in der Schrift am meisten verkörpert und ohne persönliche Merkmale ist. Hier bei dieser Karte aber wurde die Neuland-Type verwendet, ohne störend zu wirken. Mit solchen Experimenten heisst es aber vorsichtig sein. **B** Was soll denn nun aus den vielen anderen schönen Schriften werden, wenn wirklich die neue Kunst um sich greift? **A** Bisher haben die Groteskschriften ungestört in der Ecke gelegen, und nun werden sie eben mal dran kommen. Ist das nicht ein gerechter Ausgleich? **B** Ach, darum ist wohl der Text der Beilage auch gleich so gesetzt, ich meine in Grotesk. Vielleicht gar aus Sympathie? — **A** O, Sie alter Zyniker! Hier kam es doch auf eine ruhige, möglichst kräftige Type an, welche die Beispiele gut hervortreten lässt. **B** Na, klotzig genug sieht sie auch aus. **A** Aber gut in der Flächenwirkung. Wie gefällt Ihnen denn die Aufmachung dieser Beilage in der neuen Art? Jedenfalls ein Mittelweg, der auch für Prospekte usw. gut geeignet wäre. **B** Nun ja, aber ich weiss nicht, hübsch ist anders. **A** Ich finde gerade, dass sich die Seiten mit den Ecken ganz gut ausnehmen. Es liegt Abwechslung darin. **B** Ja, im Fahrten- und Abenteuerbuch liegt auch Abwechslung, ein Bild so und eins so. Ich kann nicht sagen, dass das „sachlich" ist. **A** Freilich hatte auch ich mir gedacht, dass Tschichold andere Wege der Buchkunst finden würde. Vielleicht hat er sich bewusst bezähmt; vielleicht hat auch die Büchergilde ein Wort mitgesprochen. **B** Die werden sowieso am Umsatz der Bücher den „Erfolg" (?) merken! **A** Sie meinen wohl, dass durch die neue Ausstattung die Zahl der Mitglieder steigt? **B** Das wollen wir erst mal sehen! **A** Nun hören Sie mal. Falls Sie auch Lust haben sollten, sich mal in Konstruktivismus zu versuchen, will ich Ihnen ein paar Thesen mit auf den Weg geben: I. Typographie kann unter Umständen Kunst sein. II. Gestaltung ist Wesen aller Kunst, die typographische Gestaltung ist nicht Abmalen des textlichen Inhalts. III. Auch die nichtbedruckten Stellen sind positive Werte. IV. Qualität der Type bedeutet Einfachheit und Schönheit. Die Einfachheit schliesst in sich Klarheit, eindeutige, zweckentsprechende Form, Verzicht auf allen entbehrlichen Ballast. Schönheit bedeutet gutes Ausbalancieren der Fläche. Die Forderung an die Typographie ist — **B** Hören Sie auf, mir wird ganz schlecht! **A** Schön! Für heute wollen wir dieses Thema abbrechen, beherzigen Sie meine Worte und verwerten Sie das Gute des „Elementaren".

**B** Eigentlich war es überhaupt Unfug, sich darüber noch lange zu unterhalten und vier Seiten kostbares Papier zu vergeuden, denn wir stehen ja heute mitten im Konstruktivismus, und es wird nicht lange dauern, bis auch diese Sensation ihr Ende gefunden hat. Denn so war's und ist's noch in der Welt: Im steten Wechsel liegt ja der Reiz des Lebens. **A** Ei, Donnerwetter, Sie sprechen ja so geistreich und verständig! — Gewiss vereinbart sich nicht alles im Konstruktivismus mit unseren bisherigen Anschauungen über Typographie, aber die für ihn erbrachten Begründungen sind nicht ohne weiteres von der Hand zu weisen. Der grösste Teil seiner Widersacher stützt sich meistens auf unbestimmte Gefühle. Wollen wir doch froh sein, dass wir aus der „elementaren typographie" neue Anregungen und Gedanken gewonnen haben, die leider oft in ganz falscher Verkennung der inneren Zusammenhänge weidlich ausgenutzt werden und so bei dem kritischen Beschauer ein nicht immer befriedigendes Gefühl auslösen. **B** Jedenfalls hat man um die neue Art Satzgruppierung, die man plötzlich mit „Kunst" bezeichnet, viel zuviel Wesens gemacht. Drum sei auch der Debatte ein Punkt gesetzt.

**BERATUNGEN UND ENTWÜRFE WERBEDRUCKE**

**GEORG KLEMM NICOLAISTR. 22 FERNRUF 35308**

**REKLAME DRESDEN—A. 16**

GESCHÄFTSKARTE ENTWURF HANS MENKE DRESDEN

ELECTRICITEIT BOUWT STEDEN

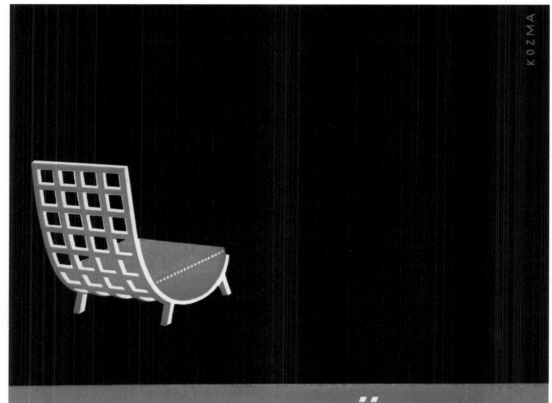

KOZMA

EINZELMÖBEL
UND NEUZEITLICHE
RAUMKUNST
HERAUSGEGEBEN
VON ALEXANDER
KOCH DARMSTADT

TYPOGRAPHICAL SIGNETS

School of decorative Art, Stuttgart, Professor Veit. Signets
composed of brass rules and typographical borders.

# FORUM

maandblad voor architectuur en gebonden kunsten

12
1953

---

**KESTNER-GESELLSCHAFT**
E.V. HANNOVER
KÖNIGSTRASSE 8

WINTER

**P**ROGRAMM

**1928-1929**

---

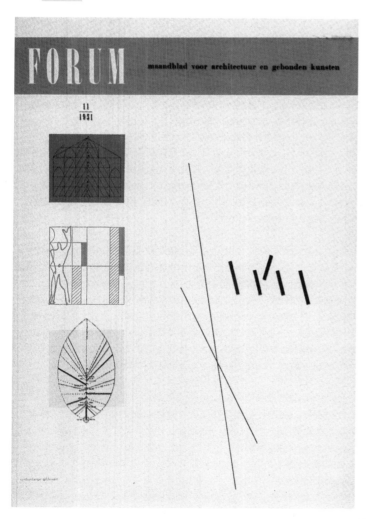

# FORUM

maandblad voor architectuur en gebonden kunsten

11
1951

---

**DER VORBILDLICHE WERBEDRUCK**

А Б В Г Д Е

Ж З И К Л М

Н О П Р С Т

У Ф Х Ц Ч Щ

Ъ Ы Ь Э Ю Я

# Таб. I.    К Проблеме Композиции:

И. Клюн. 1942 г.

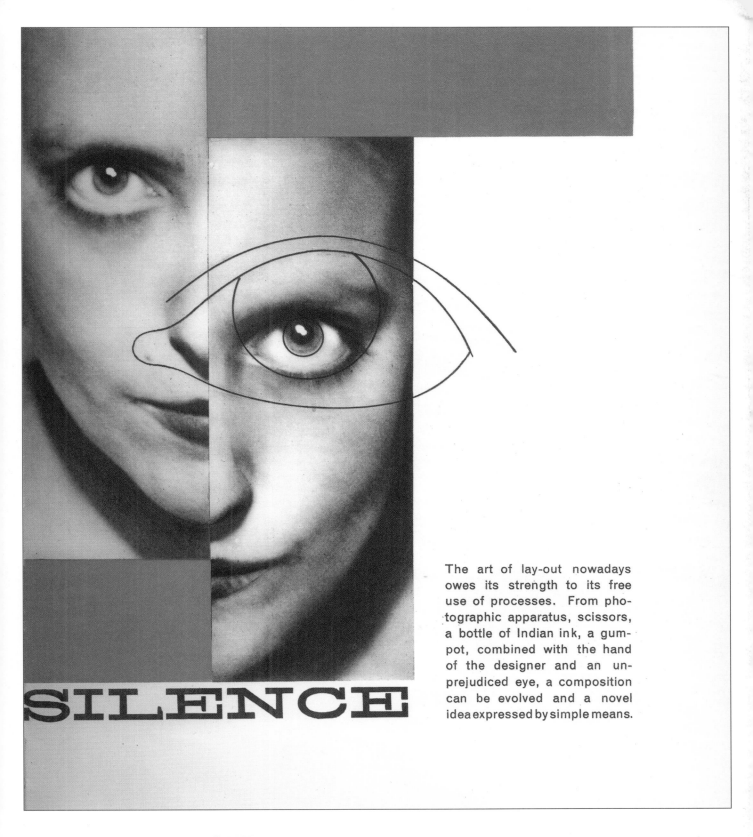

The art of lay-out nowadays owes its strength to its free use of processes. From photographic apparatus, scissors, a bottle of Indian ink, a gum-pot, combined with the hand of the designer and an unprejudiced eye, a composition can be evolved and a novel idea expressed by simple means.

SILENCE

# THE ART OF LAYOUT

*Mise en Page: The Theory and Practice of Lay-out*, by A. Tolmer, was published by *The Studio* magazine in 1932. The genius of the booklet was to instruct by example, and its texts were models of modernist economy and grace. The virtues it sought to inculcate were those of simplicity, balance, clarity of expression, and freedom from preconceptions on the use of materials and processes. Apart from its exemplary value as a design manual what gives *Mise en Page* an undeniable poignancy is the conviction it professes, in text and design, in the necessity to civilised life of principled thought and humane feeling in good practice. For Tolmer, as for Wittgenstein, it seems, "ethics and aesthetic are one".

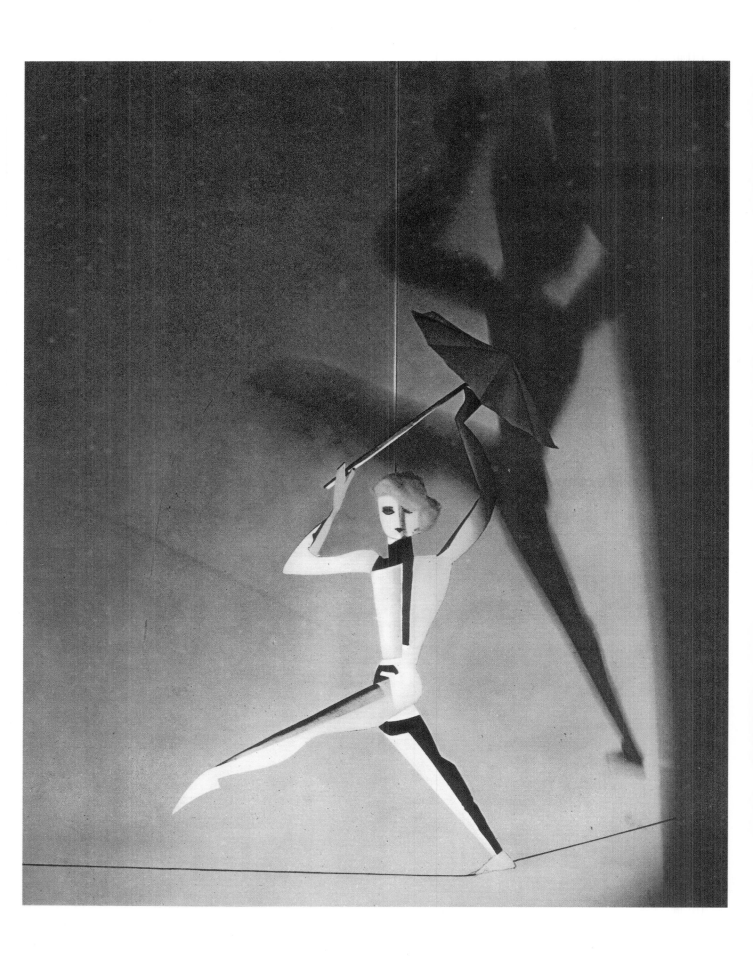

## PREFACE

Like skating or walking the tight-rope, the art of lay-out is an art of balance.

It cannot however be expressed merely as a mathematical calculation. The tight-rope walker steadies herself with her parasol rather than with the aid of a formula. The sense of stability; the right and the wrong way of doing anything; the amount of air that enables the earth to breathe; the amount of sleep that permits of the greatest activity during the day; the most satisfactory way of combining the elements of a theatre-set, the page of a book or a poster; all these things are essentially a matter of feeling.

The feelings of mankind are unaffected by the change of ideas, constructive and destructive by turns, which accompany each phase of history. Since the earliest times known to us, love, hate, joy, suffering and religion have exercised a constant influence. Every age and every civilization, therefore, must be guided by these basic impulses and the works produced under their influence, in order to test, control, and correct its own balance.

**S**o, considering the past, we might have written simply an historical study of the kind of balance represented by the art of lay-out. But this we have wished to avoid. If an historical evolution may be traced in the series of illustrations here reproduced it will not be by any means complete.

**A**n investigation has been made into the origins of the art of lay-out. The part played by the shape of text in a lay-out has been demonstrated by reference to various types of ancient writing. The links between letterpress, ornament, and architecture have been pointed out. Points of comparison between modes of lay-out used in different countries and at different periods have been established. The sole aim, however, has been that of providing rich materials for the modern method of approach.

**I**t is always a difficult matter for the professional tennis-player to discuss his game. But this is not a series of lessons in lay-out. We wish to immerse our readers in the subject and to prime them with information which will enable them to infuse fresh life and a continually changing novelty into their practice of it.

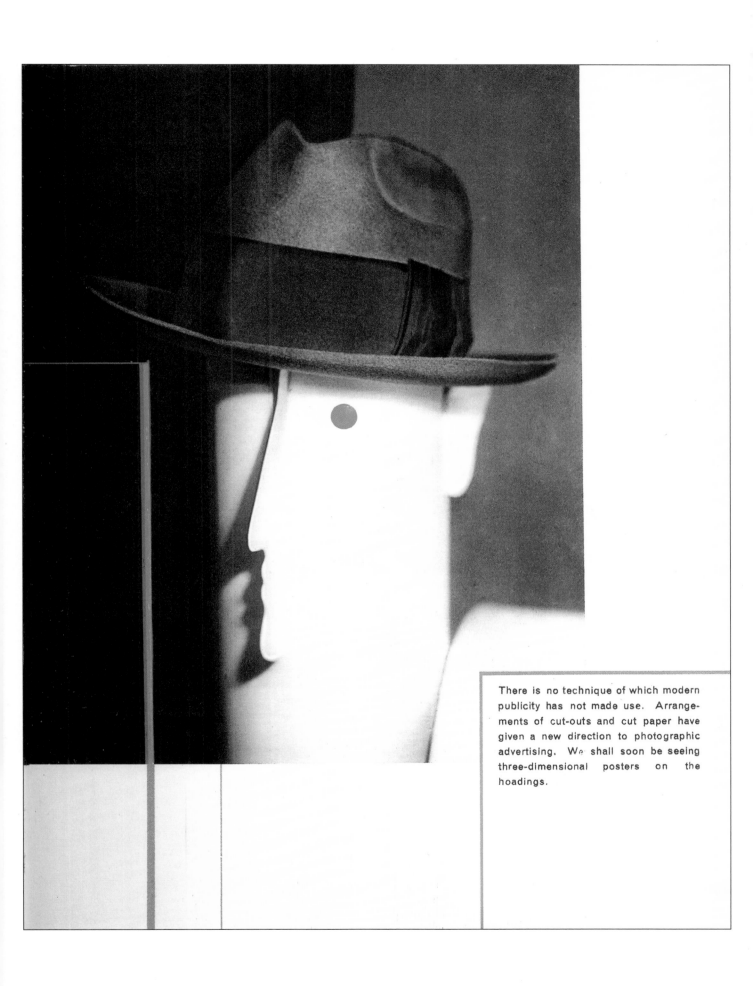

There is no technique of which modern publicity has not made use. Arrangements of cut-outs and cut paper have given a new direction to photographic advertising. We shall soon be seeing three-dimensional posters on the hoadings.

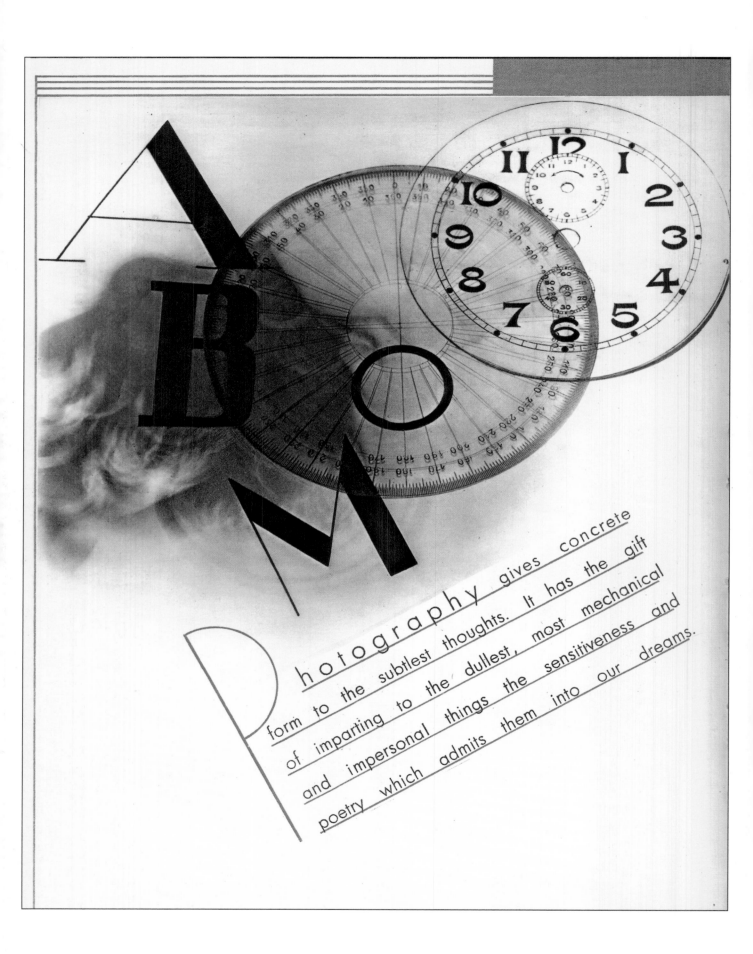

**A B O M P**hotography gives concrete form to the subtlest thoughts. It has the gift of imparting to the dullest, most mechanical and impersonal things the sensitiveness and poetry which admits them into our dreams.

# Е. ПАВЛОВ

# ВАЛЬС ПАМЯТИ СКРЯБИНА

## для фортепиано

E. PAWLOW.
valse

A LA
mémoire de
*Scriàbine.*

Государственное Музыкальное Издательство.

МОСКВА 1922.

TESA

VETRO FLEX

HEBERLEIN

+GF+

LABEL

# SOCIETEIT voor CULTUREELE SAMENWERKING

## EXCELSIOR THEATER
### ZEESTRAAT

## GASTVOORSTELLINGEN

## DIE JUNGE TRUPPE
## (BERLIN)

## 18 TOT 23 JANUARI 1931
## DER ANDERE
### VON MIGUEL DE UNAMUNO
### DEUTSCH VON OTTO BUCK
#### DRAMA IN DREI AKTEN MIT EINEM EPILOG

DER ANDERE . . . . . GILLIS van RAPPARD

LAURA . . . . . . . . . . ELLEN DAGMAR

DIAMIANA . . . . . . . . . . SYBIL RARES

ERNESTO. . . . . . . . EMILIO CARGHER

AVITO . . . . . . . . . . . . . HANS ALVA

DIE AMME. . . . . . . . . ERIKA KRISTEN

### REGIE: GILLIS van RAPPARD

PRIJZEN der PLAATSEN

ZAAL 1e DEEL FL. 3.00 ZAAL 2e DEEL FL. 2.50

ZAAL 3e DEEL en BALCON FL. 1.25

PLAATSEN TE BESPREKEN DAGELIJKS

AAN HET GEBOUW VAN 10 TOT 16 UUR

VAN 24 TOT 31 JANUARI
DIE QUADRATUR DES KREISES
LUSTSPIEL von VAL: KATAJEW

ONTWERP V. HUSZAR

VWMNK

OCSQGA

XYZIEFL

UDBRP

JTH;,!?:

गिनती ۳۲ گنتی

Published by : INDIAN BOOK DEPOT, DELHI-110 006.
Printed at INDIAN ART PRESS, NEW DELHI-110 064.

Publishers:
**INDIAN BOOK DEPOT**
2937, Bahadur Garh Rd.
Delhi-110006

Printers:
**INDIAN ART PRESS**
A/6, Mayapuri,
New Delhi-110064.

A<sub>A</sub> B<sub>b</sub> C<sub>c</sub> D<sub>d</sub> E<sub>E</sub> F<sub>f</sub> G<sub>g</sub>

H<sub>H</sub> I<sub>i</sub> J<sub>j</sub> K<sub>k</sub> L<sub>l</sub> M<sub>M</sub> N<sub>N</sub>

O<sub>O</sub> P<sub>P</sub> Q<sub>Q</sub> R<sub>R</sub> S<sub>S</sub> T<sub>T</sub> U<sub>U</sub>

V<sub>V</sub> W<sub>W</sub> X<sub>X</sub> Y<sub>y</sub> Z<sub>Z</sub>

1234567890

1234567890

ABCDE
FGHIJK
LMNOPQ
RSTUV
WXYZ

59, Page from *Arts et Métiers Graphiques*
(Deberny and Peignot, Paris, 1930s).
Courtesy David Batterham

60  Top left: Koishi Kiyoshi, cover for *Shoka-Shinkei (Sensitivity of the early summer)* Japan,
1933. Private collection.
Top right:, B. Titov, cover for *Nonsense* by V.
Woodward, (GIZ, USSR, 1927).
Courtesy Misha Anikst.
Bottom left: poster for the review *Lacerba*,
designer unknown, Italy, 1914. Private collection.
Bottom right: cover for *Filmova' Dramata*,
screenplays by Louis Delluc, (Ladislav Kuncir V
Praza Czechoslovakia, 1925). Private collection

61  Joost Schmidt, Condensed grotesque typeface
with construction details and variants of single
figures, the Netherlands, 1926.
Courtesy Richard Hollis

62  Printer's advertisement from
*Gebrauchsgraphik*, Germany, 1930s

63  Top: from a promotional folder for the typeface
*Erbar*, Ludwig and Mayer, Germany, 1930s.
Courtesy Royal College of Art Library (photograph
by Dominic Sweeney).
Bottom: from a promotional folder for the printers
Gebr. Hartmann, Germany, 1930. Collection
Redstone Press

64  Ladislav Sutnar, covers for books by George
Bernard Shaw, Czechoslovakia, early-1930s.
Courtesy Museum of Decorative Arts, Prague

65  Typeface from the *Signwriter's Manual of
Typefaces* by Richard Pípal, Czechoslovakia, 1956.
Collection Redstone Press

66  Typeface designed for use on buildings by
Edward Wright, UK, 1965. Courtesy the
Department of Typography and Graphic
Communication at The University of Reading

67  Page from *Hoffmann's Schriftatlas*, (Julius
Hoffmann Verlag, Germany, 1930).
Private collection

68  Back cover of *Gebrauchsgraphik*, Germany,
1926. Courtesy Gutenberg Museum, Mainz

69  Page from *Buffon Alphabet des Oiseaux*
(Pellerin and Cie, Paris, 1890).
Courtesy Pentagram

70  Typeface based on Standard Light Extended,
Berthold Typefounders, Early 20th Century.
Private collection

71  Jan Tschichold, film poster for Abel Gance's
*Napoleon*, 1926. (photograph by Dominic
Sweeney). Courtesy Royal College of Art Library

72  Cover of Gebrauchsgraphik,
Germany, 1930s, designer unknown.
Courtesy The Gutenberg-Museum, Mainz

73  Logos from an Italian type manufacturer's
catalogue, c.1950. Courtesy David Wakefield

74  Photomontage by Paul Schuitema,
Netherlands, 1928. Courtesy Merrill C. Berman
Collection, New York

75  Typeface from the album *Schriften, Lettering,
Ecritures*, 1940s, designer unknown. Courtesy
Klingspoor Museum, Germany

76  Back cover of *XXth Century*, designer
unknown, (English edition Christmas, 1938).
Courtesy Brian Webb Collection

79  Mauricio Amster poster for *Cartilla Escolar
Antifascista* (Ministry of Public Information Madrid,
1937), "The Cultural Militias Fight Fascism by
Combating Ignorance". Private collection

80/84  Pages from the *Antifascist Schoolbook*,
design and montages by Mauricio Amster,
photographs by José val del Omar and José
Calandin, Spain, 1937. Courtesy Lutz Becker

87  Cover for *Sinopsis* by Miguel Prieto,
Mexico, 1953. Courtesy Xavier Bermúdez

88  Miguel Prieto, typography for book covers,
poster and newspaper, Mexico, 1950s. Courtesy
Xavier Bermúdez

89  Miguel Prieto, poster for treatment of
alcoholism, Mexico c.1950.
Courtesy Xavier Bermúdez

90  Paul Renner, preliminary drawing for the
typeface *Futura*, Germany, 1925.
Private collection

91  Wladyslaw Strzeminski, cover for *Z Ponad*
by Julian Przbos, Poland, 1930.
Courtesy Merrill C. Berman Collection, New York

92  A. Kruchenykh, drawing from *Learn Artists*, Russia, 1917. Private collection

93  Russian block alphabet, designer known, date unknown. Courtesy David Hillman

94  Alphabet from *Methods of Lettering* by Fridrich Moravcik, Bratislava, 1975. Collection Redstone Press

95  Top left: cover of *Zlom* by Konstantin Biebel, design by Karel Teige, Czechoslovakia, 1928. © Estate of Karel Teige. Private collection. Top right: cover of *Diabolo* by Viteslav Nezval design by H. V. Obrtel, Czechoslovakia, 1926. Private collection. Bottom: typographical compositions for *Zlom* by Karel Teige, Czechoslovakia, 1928. Private collection

96  Political poster design by Marinetti, Italy, 1930s. Private collection. © DACS 2002

97/98  Typeface, designer unknown, mid-1900s. Private collection

99  Cover of *Campo de Grafico*, designer unknown, Italy, 1939

100  Gothic wood letter, designer unknown, UK, c.1837

101  Ilya Zdanevich, title page of *Zohna and Brides*, Russia c.1925. Courtesy Misha Anikst

102  Cover of *Le Mot*, design by Paul Iribe, France, 1915. Courtesy David Batterham

103  Typeface from the *Signwriter's Manual of Typefaces*, by Richard Pípal, Czechoslovakia, 1956. Collection Redstone Press

104  Symbols from *Typogane*, typefounders' catalogue, Germany, c.1933. Courtesy Jan Solpera

105  *Les Catalanes*, a typeface design by Enric Crous-Vidal (never produced) from Caractère Noël, Spain, 1952. Courtesy Fundación Tipográfia Bauer Spain

106/107  Pages from the Marsh Stencil Machine Co. catalogue, USA c.1947. Courtesy collection of Eric Finkel

108  From the *Lettering Manual* by Jan Sembera, Czechoslovakia, 1938. Collection Redstone Press

109  Josef Síma, cover of *Love Poems* by Otakar Storch-Marien, Czechoslovakia, 1928

110  Max Burchartz, title page of leaflets for *The Motley Square No. 2*, Germany, 1924. Courtesy Merrill C. Berman Collection, New York

111  From promotional folder for *Futura* typeface, 1930s. Courtesy Klingspoor Museum, Germany

112  Herbert Bayer, Bauhaus leaflet, Germany, 1928. Courtesy Merrill C. Berman Collection, New York. © DACS 2002

113  Symbols from *Graphic News*, Germany, 1939. Courtesy Verlag Hermann Schmidt, Mainz

114  Fortunata Depero, collage, Italy, 1928. © DACS 2002

117  Eye chart instruction cards for patients with hearing difficulties, F. C. Cooper (London mid 20th Century. )

117/123  Photographs and eye test charts from *Eye and Instruments: Nineteenth-century ophthalmological instruments in the Netherlands* by Isolde den Tonkelaar, Harold E. Henkes and Gijsbert K. van Leersum (1996). Courtesy of, BV Uitgeverij De Bataafsche Leeuw, Van Soeren and Co. Amsterdam

118  Snellen optotypes (post-1875)

119  Snellen optotype Left: For testing astigmatism (c.1872). Right: Open-sided squares for non-readers (1874)

120  Breslau ophthalmologist Wolffberg's optotypes for children featuring figures and signs (1892)

121  Snellen charts featuring letter types and Snellen's fan for determining the direction of astigmatism (c.1875)

122  Left: Optotypes in Japanese lettering designed by Ito Gempak who worked with Snellen from 1870 to 1880 (1873) Right: Optotype in Gothic lettering published by H. Peters (Berlin 1873)

123   Left: Snellen chart, and Right: Snellen chart with E-figures for non-readers (both post-1875)

124   Hand operated colour-mills for testing colour recognition (Left: 1860 Right: c.1875 to 1900)

127   Chinese ideogram with two birds, 18th Century. Courtesy Fang Chen

128   Cover of "Lettres": Arts et Métiers Graphiques (Deberny and Peignot, Paris, 1948). Collection Redstone Press

129/130   Fregio Mecano, typeface from a typefounders' catalogue Italy c.1930. Courtesy Pentagram

131   Cover of Cobra Norato (Nheengatu du margem esquerda do Amazonas), designer unknown, Brazil, 1931. Private collection

132   Publicity announcement for Futura typeface "The type of our time" design by Paul Renner, Germany, 1930, (reproduced in Gebrauchsgraphik, Germany, 1930). Courtesy Gutenberg-Museum, Mainz

133   Page from Hoffmann's Schriftatlas, Julius Hoffmann, Verlag, Germany, 1930. Private collection

134   Typeface with two styles, France, date unknown. Private collection

135   Advertisement from Arts et Métiers Graphiques, (Deberny and Peignot, Paris, 1930s). Private collection

136   Aleksandr Rodchenko, Still Life with Leica, photograph, Russia, 1930. Courtesy Alexander Lavrentiev, The Rodchenko / Stepanova Archive, Moscow

137   Aleksandr Rodchenko, front cover of Conversation with the Finance Inspector about Poetry by Vladimir Mayakovsky, Russia, 1926. Courtesy, Alexander Lavrentiev, The Rodchenko / Stepanova Archive, Moscow

138   Top: wrapper for a joke ink-blot made of tin, Germany c.1890. Collection Redstone Press. Bottom: from a typefounders' manual, USA, c.1900. Collection Redstone Press

139   Edward Wright, drawing for a typeface, UK, 1965. Courtesy Department of Typography and Graphic Communication at The University of Reading

140   Designs for letterheads reproduced in Typografia XXXVIII, Czechoslovakia, 1930s. Courtesy Museum of Decorative Arts, Prague

141   Karel Sourek, cover for Jazz by E. F. Burian, Czechoslovakia, 1928. Collection Redstone Press

142   Cover of Arts et Métiers Graphiques (Deberny and Peignot Paris, 1938). Collection Redstone Press

143   Signwriter's alphabet, from the Rotterdamsche Schilderschool (compiled by A. R. van der Burg, the Netherlands early-1900s). Courtesy Jan Tholenaar Collection, Amsterdam

144   Hand-drawn typeface, designer unknown, date unknown. Private collection

145   Advertisement for Wurzburg Brothers (1930s) from The Encyclopedia of the Packaging Industry, (Breskin and Charlton Publishing Corporation, New York, 1936). Courtesy Pentagram

146   From The Manual of Typefaces by Richard Pípal, Czechoslovakia, 1956. Collection Redstone Press

147   Karel Teige, Untitled, print with watercolor, Czechoslovakia, 1927. Collection Merrill C. Berman, New York. © The Estate of Karel Teige

148   Top: cigarette pack designs ("Miss Mend" was the title of a popular series of detective novels) designers unknown except Top right: design by Aleksandr Rodchenko. Courtesy Misha Anikst. Bottom: poster advertising cigarettes. Courtesy Misha Anikst.

149   Russian alphabet probably based on Bodoni, Russia, c.1890. Private collection

150   Specimens of embossing by Waterhouse Brothers and Layton Ltd. UK, 1890. Private collection

151,152,161,162   Design for end-papers by Hiang Kee, UK, 1980. Collection Redstone Press

153/160  Typeface designs from signwriter's manuals from, *Modèles de Lettres sur des fonds differents*, and *Modèles de Lettres pour peintres en bâtiments* (France early-1900s). Courtesy Collinge and Clark

163  E. Di Vavalcanti, cover design for the journal *Joaquim No. 15*, Brazil, 1947 Private collection

164  Logotypes from *The Typeface Handbook* by E. Beaufort, Czechoslovakia c.1935. Courtesy Museum of Decorative Arts, Prague

165  Top: typeface from signwriters, manual, Czechoslovakia, 1930s. Collection, Redstone Press. Bottom: Frantisek Zelenka '*Three Jazz Reviews*', poster, 1930, Czechoslovakia. Courtesy Museum of Decorative Arts, Prague

166  Menu, designer unknown, from *Arts et Métiers Graphiques*, (Deberny and Peignot, Paris, 1930s). Collection Redstone Press

167  Typeface, designer unknown, UK, c.1890. Collection Redstone Press

168  Typefaces designed by Paul Carlyle and Guy Oring from *Letters and Lettering* (McGraw-Hill Book Co. USA, 1938). Courtesy Brian Webb Collection

169  Advertisement for Ever Ready Labels from *The Encyclopedia of the Packaging Industry* (Breskin and Charlton Publishing Corporation, New York, 1936). Courtesy Pentagram

170/171  Two versions of typeface Patrona Grotesk, designer unknown, date unknown, Czechoslovakia. Courtesy Jan Solpera

172  Flourishes designed by Enric Crous-Vidal, Spain, 1953. Courtesy Fundación Tipográfica Bauer, Barcelona

173  Typeface designed by Enric Crous-Vidal, date unknown, Spain. Courtesy Fundación Tipográfica Bauer, Barcelona

174  Michel Leiris, *Amour*, from *Glossary: Where My Gloss Err*, Paris, 1939. Private collection

175  Lowercase Slender Roman letters from *Hoffmann's Schriftatlas*, (Julius Hoffmann Verlag Germany, 1930). Private collection

176  A. M. Cassandre, *Bifur*, alphabet, France, 1929. Courtesy Klingspoor Museum, Offenbach

177  Jan Tschichold, poster for opera, *Casanova*, Germany, 1920s, from Gebrauchsgraphik, 1928. Courtesy Gutenberg-Museum, Mainz

178  Top left: cover of issue of *Campo Grafico* dedicated to Italian Futurism, design by Saladin, Italy, 1942. Private collection.
Top right: cover of the issue of *Campo Grafico* dedicated to Italian Futurism, design by Bona, Italy, 1939. Private collection.
Bottom left: cover of *Denki Ningyo* (Italian: Fantocci elettrici) designer unknown, Tokyo, 1925. Private collection.
Bottom right: announcement of the death of Umberto Boccione in *L'Italia Futurista*, Italy, 1916, (design by Giacomo Balla). Private collection

179  Gothic Special wood letters designed at the Hamilton Company, USA, c.1910, from *American Wood Type 1828 to 1900* by Rob Roy Kelly, (Da Capo Press USA, 1977)

180  Typeface design by Morris Fuller Benton, USA, 1935. Private collection

181  Miroslav Ponc, cover design for Dr. J. Brandenberger 1877 to 1927 (Akrostichon, Prague, 1927). Courtesy City Gallery, Prague

182  From "*Lettres*": Arts et Métiers Graphiques (Deberny and Peignot, Paris, 1948). Collection Redstone Press

183  Robert Michel, Collage, 1927, Germany. Collection Merrill C. Berman, New York

184  Jan Tschichold, instructional page from *The New Typography*, Germany, 1928. Collection Mel Gooding

185/186  Pages from *Typographic News*, Germany, 1926. Courtesy Verlag Hermann Schmidt, Mainz

187  Top: Piet Zwart, from N. C. W. Catalogue, Netherlands, 1928. Collection Merrill C. Berman, New York. © DACS 2002.
Bottom: Jan Tschichold, covers for the book *Fototek* nos. 1 and 2, Berlin, 1930. Collection Merrill C. Berman, New York

188  Promotional brochure, design Kozma c.1930. Collection Merrill C. Berman, New York

189   Page from *Hoffmann's Schriftatlas*, (Julius Hoffmann Verlag Germany, 1930).
Private collection

190   Friedrich Vordemberge-Gildewart designs.
Top left/bottom left: covers for the architectural magazine *Forum*, the Netherlands, 1953 to 1951.
Top right: Prospectus for Kestner-Gesellschaft, Hanover, 1928.
Bottom right: cover for advertising prospectus for the H. Osterwald Printing Works, Hanover, 1927, from *Vordemberge-Gildewart: The Complete Works*, Prestel Verlag.
© The Vordemberge-Gildewart Foundation

191   Stencil alphabet, designer unknown, Russia, c.1920

192   I. V. Kliun, watercolor chart from unpublished instructional volume, Moscow, 1942, (ex. Costakis Collection)

195/200   Pages from *Mise En Page: The Theory and Practice of Lay-out* by A. Tolmer (The Studio Ltd, London, 1932). Courtesy The Department of Typography and Graphic Communication at The University of Reading

203   Liubov Popova, cover of *Valse* by E Pavlov, Russia, 1922. Private collection

204   Top left: cover of *Integral*, designer unknown, Romania, 1925. Private collection.
Top right: cover of *Blok*, designer unknown, Poland, 1926. Private collection.
Bottom left: collage poster design by Mihailo S. Petrov for Zenit exhibition, Yugoslavia, 1924. Private collection.
Bottom right: cover design by M. H. Maxy for *Contimporanul*, Romania, 1924.
Private collection

205   Alphabet design by Cehonin, Russia, 1925. Private collection

206   Symbols from *Trade Marks and Symbols*, (Graphis, Zurich, 1948)

207   Theatre poster design by Vilmos Huszar, Berlin, 1931. Courtesy Merrill C. Berman Collection, New York

208   Alphabet design by William Dressler, c.1950, from *Lettering Art in Modern Use* (Reinhold Publishers, USA, 1952)

209   Photograph of printer-designers, photographer unknown, from *Schriftenproben*, design by Walter Cyliax, (Gebr. Fretz Ab Zurich, 1933). Courtesy Brian Webb Collection

210   Top: lettering, design by K. C. Aryan from *Calligraphy and Symbols*, India, 1966.
Bottom: "Japanese-style" lettering, date unknown. Courtesy Dover Publications

211   Top: front and back covers of school-book, India c.1955. Private collection.
Bottom: matchbox label, Japan, 1930. Collection Redstone Press

212   A. M. Cassandre, poster for Florent pastilles, published Hachard and Cie, Paris, 1930s. Private collection

213   A. M. Cassandre, *Peignot* typeface. Paris, 1937. Private collection

214   *Didot* typeface, France, c.1810. Private collection

215   From *Le Mot*, design by Paul Iribe, Paris, 1930s. Private collection

# REDSTONE PRESS

publishes the Redstone Diary and one or two new books each year

these are available through our website at

## www.redstonepress.co.uk

or please write for a catalogue to:

# 7a St Lawrence Terrace London W10 5SU

telephone (44) 20 7352 1594 or fax (44) 20 7352 8749